H·I·G·H
TOUCH

The New Materialism
in Design

Robert Janjigian

With Laura J. Haney

Foreword by Ivy Ross

E. P. Dutton
New York

A RUNNING HEADS BOOK

Published in the United States by E. P. Dutton,
a division of NAL Penguin Inc.,
2 Park Avenue, New York, N.Y. 10016.

Library of Congress Catalog Card Number: 87-71323
ISBN: 0-525-24572-3 (cloth)
ISBN: 0-525-48340-3 (DP)

HIGH TOUCH
was conceived and produced by Running Heads Incorporated
42 East 23rd Street, New York, New York 10010

Editor: Jill Herbers
Designer/Photo Researcher: Lesley Achitoff

Typeset by David E. Seham Associates
Color separations by Hong Kong Scanner Craft Company Ltd.
Printed and bound in Hong Kong by Leefung-Asco Printers Ltd.
10 9 8 7 6 5 4 3 2 1
First American Edition

For my family

ACKNOWLEDGMENTS

I would like to thank Scott Atkinson, Ileen Sheppard and the other members of the Queens Museum staff. I am also indebted to Laura J. Haney. Thanks to Running Heads: My editor Jill Herbers; Marta Hallett; and Ellen Milionis. I'd also like to thank Cyril Nelson at Dutton. Others who worked on the book and deserve thanks are Cornelia Guest, Eileen Schlesinger, and Lesley Achitoff for her terrific design. Deborah Morosini deserves special thanks, as she encouraged and listened to me while writing—from the beginning. Bruce Keiser provided a needed break while I was in Atlanta. Ivy Ross, Marc Lieberman, Barry Dean, Julie Radin, Jan Lindstrom, Julia Hull, Mark Hemphill, Brenda Segal, Nayana Currimbhoy, Michael Murdoch and all the artists and designers and photographers should know that their help was appreciated.

CONTENTS

CHAPTER 1 ◆ **THE NEW MATERIALISM**   1

CHAPTER 2 ◆ **SEATING**   11

CHAPTER 3 ■ **TABLES**   29

CHAPTER 4 ◆ **STORAGE**   47

CHAPTER 5 ◀ **LIGHTING**   59

CHAPTER 6 ■ **SETTINGS**   73

CHAPTER 7 ◆ **OBJECTS**   91

ACCESSORIES   92
WEARABLES   104

SOURCES   114
BIBLIOGRAPHY   115
INDEX   116
PHOTO CREDITS   118

FOREWORD

In a departure from previous decades, design today has become a reflective process, going beyond pure function to take into account experience, knowledge, and emotions. Objects being designed now are seeking new possibilities of communication to transmit our responses, feelings, and aspirations. No longer are the simple technical functions of furniture and objects the only consideration; the pieces' expressive value is important as well. Materials, texture, pattern, and color are just some of the factors that contribute to this new means of expression.

Furniture design has always reflected the needs of the existing culture. In the space-conscious 1960s, for example, designers offered space-saving and economical furniture such as convertibles and inflatable plastic chairs. Today's furniture designers, however, address far more serious needs that have not been generally recognized before. While they seek to satisfy pragmatic needs, their concerns are also with renewing humanity. At the same time, they are exploring their own passions and imaginations. The intent is to use furniture and accessories to individualize interior environments fully.

Furniture and objects designers now choose from a palette of materials in much the same way that a painter chooses color. Often, materials are selected for their value to the imagery of a piece, rather than to explore a current technological breakthrough. And when the same materials are used by different designers, the vast individual approaches are evident.

Materials such as plywood, steel, aluminum, and plastics have been used in modern furniture since the late 1900s, and were featured in many important pieces thereafter. On occasion a search for new ways to use materials spurred the development of new commercial processes such as plywood and laminate. At other times the emergence of new equipment or technology encouraged the acceptance of a manufacturing technique that was previously impractical. This approach to design suited the machine age, with both designer and manufacturer fully exploiting the new capabilities of mass production. It allowed for the emergence of the Bauhaus, whose aim it was to standardize formality and reorganize the environment along rational lines.

But beginning in the seventies these standard products became alienating and terrifying. Offices incorporated technology for its efficiency, ignoring its insensitivity to local character and communication between workers. The industrial revolution had been too rapid and too complex for both the public and the artist.

Neither has what is called the new technology solved

that problem. It has just produced more items thought to please everyone and offend no one from designs made for a kind of neutral taste of society that no longer really exists. As Daniel Weil states, "The new technology is said to be revolutionary, but a revolution has to be a revolution of ideas. The new technology is not like that. It is just making our old mechanical ideas faster than before."

In fact, it seems as though mass producers are trying to individualize their products by offering the same guts in many different outside colors. Tactile controls and eccentric cosmetic colors such as mint green and pink are seen in everything from TV's to radios. What these manufacturers are not recognizing is that the need for individuality goes much deeper than packaging.

Because of this void in mass production and as a reaction against what happened in previous eras, people are seeking images and fantasy in both products and architecture. For furniture and objects they are turning to the alternatives offered by smaller industries and individual artists and designers. The environment has become a social theater. The objects that we once took for granted are becoming a means for communication. These products, like our current society, display a sense of individualism and risk-taking.

Italy, which a few years back tested the notion of beauty through bizarre and challenging designs from the Memphis design collaborative, no longer is the dominant creative force in design. It is not in a position to produce pieces with the raw directness that is needed today. This factor has contributed to the surge of creative energy entering the world furniture market from Paris, Barcelona, the United States, and England. High Touch has contributions from all these places, but it is in the United States that the movement is most aggressive.

High Touch artists and designers are no longer making a lamp, for example, purely for decoration, but are instead changing the idea of a lamp. With materials design, many of these new objects are free expressions independent from function. This work is emerging because people are looking for surprising additions to their environment that reflect their individuality. In fact, much of the work carries a message that the creator begins and that the owner must complete. It is in this way that High Touch becomes most personal, most like art and design combined, and in many ways, most revolutionary.

Ivy Ross

1
THE NEW MATERIALISM

What Is High Touch?

The High Touch design movement has been called "the new materialism" and "Postmodern industrial posh." The initial concept of high touch was posited by John Naisbitt in his influential book, *Megatrends: Ten New Directions Transforming Our Lives.* High touch as he presented it is the reaction in all facets of life to high technology's influence. Writes Naisbitt, "Whenever new technology is introduced into society, there must be a counterbalancing human response—that is, high touch. The more high tech, the more high touch."

Of course, this affects the environment in the form of furnishings and interior design. Here the overall high touch approach involves the use of forms, materials, and intentions that lend a uniquely human touch, injecting individualized artistic and tactile elements into homes where VCR's, compact disc players, personal computers, microwave ovens, electronic exercycles, hair dryers, and other machines play an increasingly important role in everyday life.

Part of that counterbalancing has manifested itself in a return to tradition that accounts for the renewed interest in antiques and old-style craftsmanship. It encompasses everything from handmade quilts to English country style chintzes and reproductions that are mass-produced but made to seem individualized.

What happens when an artist, a sculptor, an architect, an inventor, or a designer reacts against technology and blank-box modernism is something else, and that is High Touch as defined by this book.

Colors, patterns, forms, textures, and, most importantly, choice of materials can effectively counterbalance the plethora of microchip technology and standardized parts. In this movement, there is little in terms of a unifying style or set philosophy of design. The main factor that brings these pieces together—and sets them apart—is what they are made of.

High Touch is materials-rich design, the use of elements in an unaccustomed context that encourages innovative exploration and experimentation with diverse materials, old and new. It is shapes and forms associated with previous styles of furniture and architecture being used in a new context. It is function despite form in that High Touch furnishings and furniture can mock the form while participating in it. A cement finish on a dresser says paradoxically that the dresser is a solid, important piece of furniture while poking fun at more traditional finishes.

RIGHT: In the 1950s Charles and Ray Eames experimented with plastics, producing many classic chairs for the Herman Miller company.

Above all, High Touch is designed to communicate. Its elements can startle and make humorous, metaphorical or even political statements. Paul Ludick's *Apartheid Chair*, made of chain-link fencing and a stream of different colors, is only one example. Designer Leo Blackman describes this aspect of the movement when he says, "I view my work as just another type of communication, especially when I see it in someone else's home. I realize then that there is a connection between what I was saying when making the piece and the buyer's interpretation of the piece, even if the two differ."

There is a tactile sensation here that one doesn't find in other work, so the selection of one material over another plays a crucial role in design choices and final effect. Creating a strong aesthetic with materials and forms, High Touch designs consist of things that seldom have been invited into the average living room.

Concrete, rubber, raw metals, and synthetic stone are among the broad range of materials used in lieu of conventional wood, glass, and steel. In High Touch, one looks beyond the traditional uses of things such as metals, plastic laminates, and cement. Corian, for example, has been taken off kitchen counters and used in everything from chairs to lamps to jewelry.

When two or more artists or designers choose the same material, the resulting aesthetics can be astonishingly individual depending on the approach taken. Architecturally inspired shapes and the very different craftsy—funky shapes can share the same medium.

An artist may depart entirely from the conventional use of rubber to employ it as a fresh and undiscovered structural element, such as a table leg, or as a textural sheathing that has no familiar association, as Brian Kane does when he coats a metal chair frame in rubber. The same may be said of concrete. Don Ruddy and Shane Kennedy of Furniture Club create objects such as tables that are not commonly made of concrete and retain the material's rough, chalky texture. Charles Pfister and Rex Designs, on the other hand, process cement to become less raw and less recognizable.

Aluminum, with its Modernist heritage, becomes a new material in the hands of Elizabeth Browning Jackson or Forrest Myers, while Jay Adams uses it appreciatively in its more conventional form. Steel, with its ties to the construction and automotive industries, is also manipulated and transformed. Juergen Riehm explores the finish. Richard Nonas uses rough steel to make small household objects and seating. Paul Ludick uses found metal parts in making functional furniture. This "researching of materials," as Don Ruddy describes it, is what brings High Touch much of its vitality.

Furniture that ignores or downplays function demands to be judged by different standards. The galleries that display High Touch pieces have devised names for it such as art furniture and neo/new/now furniture. In many cases, this furniture is designed *and* built by the designer or artist in a hands-on craft approach that in many cases is more like making sculpture than building furniture. Artist Paul Ludick says, "I made a conscious decision to go into furniture because I felt it was a way to incorporate the sculptural with the performance aspects of my work. My pieces are sculptures in that I am dealing with an object, and performance in terms of how the person relates to the object, the approach, how one sits down, and the comfort that is achieved or not achieved."

But artist Tucker Viemeister says, "A chair is fine to look at but it's probably even better to sit on. That's the whole problem with this being labeled art furniture—people are afraid to use it." So High Touch is really both things, bridging the gap between art and furniture. What is being created now is functional art. One cannot ignore the economics and the impact of furniture design, and the innovations that come from mass production and related technologies. Nor can one ignore the craft and design traditions of our culture. All of these factors have shaped High Touch.

The parade of "isms" that constitutes the jargon of recent art history has taught us, as viewers of contemporary art, to look beyond form and content to process, association, and concept. Understanding a work of art involves the perception that choices integral to the impact of a piece were made by its creator to communicate ideas ranging from the personal and obscure to the broadbased and universal. In the 1980s, popular interest in furniture design means that more people are judging one-of-a-kind and limited-run pieces by the same criteria used in evaluating fine art. And furniture, like sculpture, its closely related nonfunctioning sibling, offers a vast choice of medium.

Material Precedents of High Touch

It is the aggressive and nontraditional use of materials that sets High Touch apart from the way materials have been used in past movements. But elements that foreshadowed High Touch were present in varying degrees in all of the preceding styles of this century because experimentation with the materials of furniture construction played some part in each of them. In the Arts and Crafts Movement, Art Deco, De Stijl, Bauhaus, International Style, Scandinavian Modern, Pop, and High Tech, materials were explored to some degree.

New materials were invented in the twentieth century, nearly all of which have been explored and adapted for use by the design community—architects, interior designers, industrial designers, and furniture makers. At one time natural materials, such as wood, leather, stone, mined metals, and spun natural fibers, set the boundaries. With the technological advancements made throughout the century, there is a new and far broader palette with which to work. In expanding the vocabulary of home furnishings design, new forms were created that are important to the evolution of High Touch.

Historically, the incorporation of new materials into a design composition of form, color, and materials has implied a progressive, more enlightened way of thinking. But as in the field of science, "modern," in furniture design, meant that high technology was embraced and high touch (sensory or sensual), human characteristics were sacrificed. In the 1920s the experimental material of choice was tubular steel, and our best examples come from the Bauhaus school and from Ludwig Mies van der Rohe and Marcel Breuer. Adapted from its industrial and construction uses to furniture design, tubular steel became a symbol of the technological future. The shiny alternative to wood spoke of mass production and the infant Machine Age. Designers left the streamlined metallic surface unadorned to follow their aesthetic choice in renouncing ornamentation and to fulfill their design for an "honest" material. And steel could be manipulated to create new forms. Its strength and flexibility allowed for thin, sinuous silhouettes. Chair seats could be cantilevered, defying gravity and simplifying their conventional composition and structure.

Constant experimenting yielded new shapes in seating, whose curvilinear or less angular forms balanced the slim angularity of Modernist storage furniture. After all, the true function of seating is to accommodate the human anatomy in some degree of comfort.

The age of plastics in object design began with Dr. Leo Baekland and his invention, Bakelite, in the first decade of this century. Throughout the twentieth century Baekland's innovation was refined and developed into the many varieties of what we now call plastic. With each new development, the design community grew to appreciate plastic's properties: flexibility, durability, light weight, and the ability to take on color. Unconfined by tradition, architects, designers, and

LEFT: M. Clark Robertson's *Work Table* with silkscreened-marble tiles and steel base is both art and furniture.

artists could explore thoroughly new forms. And the nature of the material created a new sensory experience. Plastic could replace "proper" materials.

In the 1950s, a national preoccupation with science led to amoeboid sofas and parabola-shaped tables. In the 1960s, the fluid properties of plastic, polyester, and fiberglass inspired ribbon-like curves. And in the 1970s, formed polyfoam in varying densities allowed frames to be eliminated altogether.

Notably successful experiments into the properties and possibilities of plastic as a major structural element for seating are Charles and Ray Eames' molded fiberglass seating designs for Herman Miller Inc. in the 1940s and 1950s; in Joe Colombo's boldly colored mass-produced Kartell chairs of the 1960s and 1970s; and in the brief but memorable flirtation with inflatable plastic furniture by many Italian designers, which was essentially a Pop phenomenon. Lucite, invented in 1930, did not come into its own as a less fragile and lighter-weight substitute for glass until the early 1970s.

In between the love affair with one-piece injection-molded furniture such as Kartell chairs and seating comprised entirely of controlled density foams, was the furry-mushroom fad, a throwaway design that foreshadowed the intentional whimsy of High Touch. The fad came from the mass-market manufacturer DMI and designer Jim Peed. In two sizes and eleven colors, it was made of foam, plywood, cardboard, and fake fur at the rate of one every two minutes for 2 1/2 years. The University of Illinois at Carbondale thought enough of it to put it in a show of classic furniture along with chairs by Saarinen and Mies van der Rohe.

With the 1970s came a recognition of the High tech design interest, where awareness of the material was implicit to design expression and vocabulary. If

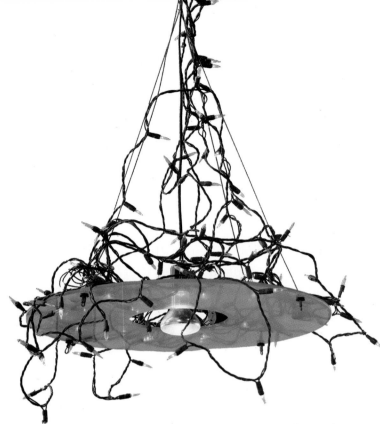

ABOVE: This hanging lamp designed by Los Angeles architect Brian A. Murphy is a funky statement of found materials: Christmas lights and glass.

we believe Emilio Ambasz's definition of high tech as the "doctrine of alternative reutilization," then High Tech has been with us to some degree since 1851, when Joseph Paxton built the Crystal Palace in London, using steel and glass and various methods developed for producing prefabricated greenhouses. A hundred years later (1949) in Santa Monica, California, the Eames house was built of stock industrial materials.

High Tech's main chroniclers Joan Kron and Suzanne Slesin delineate a marketing executive's dream, a style espoused by esteemed architects and designers of which the products were not only mass-produced but available at the retail market. The popularized High Tech style coincided with the minimalist approach to interior design, and a group of interior de-

signers and architects emerged who were immersed in an appreciation of the simple, honest approach to form in design and to the functional aspects of the materials used to make up a piece of furniture or an entire room. As with Bauhaus, the vocabulary of industry became the vocabulary for design expression. Metal deckplates for marine use appeared as wallcovering; moving-van pads became upholstery fabric; rubber-tile flooring left the airports to become kitchen flooring; glass blocks from exterior walls of factories moved to interior walls of office buildings and restaurants. Cheap corrugated cardboard was elevated to "dropdead" chic.

So, interestingly, High Tech as a style for furniture and furnishings does share some characteristics with High Touch, especially in the sense that industrial materials and objects are removed from their original contexts and given a contemporary meaning. But High Touch designers freely exchange one use for another; they manipulate materials to alter their referents.

Postmodern is the favored overall term to describe the present decade's style. But it is a misnomer, having come into favor as a convenience for critics and writers, to simplify and categorize the work of artists. The term, in fact, is essentially an assessment of what is *not* occurring in art, architecture, and design that *did* occur previously. Perhaps the term *Postmodern* has been adopted because there is no one overriding stylistic tendency that describes what is not viewed as true cutting-edge modernism.

The 1980s have brought forth a return to ornamentation as a part of design. There are increasing numbers of architects, designers, and craftsmen who clearly reject the austerity of form and the minimalism not only of the Bauhaus, but also of 1970s minimalism and High Tech and the 1950s International Style.

One example of this trend is the 1981 contemporary Italian design collaborative, Memphis, with its odd, sometimes intentionally clumsy approach to form and its particularly bold color sense, a group that tries to spark a renaissance of risk-taking, colorful furniture designs that do more to test the accepted notions of beauty than they do to make a statement about new materials. Memphis rebels against function for the sake of function and devotes itself to form for the sake of fun.

In the United States, Robert Venturi has reacted against the lack of ornamentation in architecture and furniture design for the past twenty years. Another American, Michael Graves, has been hailed as the emblem of Postmodern Neoclassical design by leading journals of interior design and architecture for his use of traditional arches, pediments, and columns combined with the gentle but intense pastels we associate with Florida Art Deco architecture.

The material-obscuring surface decoration; the use of contrasting, opposing, almost clashing colors together on the same chair, teapot, tile, or vanity table; the scattered motifs of squiggles and dots and triangles—these things entered the public vernacular in quickly produced consumer goods like paper plates, wrapping papers, and textiles. The Memphis collaborative, in evoking the angularity and bold color of Art Deco, the absurd patternings of 1940s textiles, and the colors and shapes of 1950s mass-produced Populuxe furniture and custom swimming pools, shook up the design community as it intended to do, and succeeded in awakening a greater interest in furniture with visually complex effects.

In some respects, High Touch and Memphis participate in the same aesthetic: playfulness, color, invention in shape, and interplay of texture. But Memphis looks like what it is, the sleekly professional work of professional designers in a contemporary idiom. By comparison, much of High Touch is unfinished and spontaneous—springing up everywhere from different sources—and conveys a brashness that announces that it is not only the new kid on the block, but the kid most likely to disrupt the class.

It is not just preceding styles that practitioners of High Touch design draw upon and react against, but also national economics. Economic slowdown has traditionally spurred technological advances, forcing manufacturers to invent new ways to part consumers from their money. These advances often don't reach the mass market until the nation's finances recover. For instance, television was invented in the 1920s but was not marketed until the 1940s. Increasingly, materials manufacturers turn to the artist/designer for help in making a new technology acceptable to consumers.

DuPont's Corian, a mineral/acrylic-based plastic, was promoted in the 1960s as simply a material for counter-tops. It was marketed as a more durable solution than plastic laminate, which would turn yellow and melt with heat, and easier to care for than marble, whose porosity made stains impossible to remove without professional help. Recently, Corian's designated use has been expanded as it is specified in designs for tables, chairs and lighting fixtures. Like Lucite, it has been accepted as a less fragile—in fact, bulletproof—replacement for a traditional material. It offers the durability of stone, but can be worked as easily as wood and can be translucent as well.

Celebrating twenty years in plastic laminates, the Formica Corporation introduced its new plastic surfacing material to architects and designers with an invitation to "Explore ColorCore." With its solid color through-and-through and its ability to be cold-formed into an arc, Formica executives reasoned that the best way for the potentials of ColorCore to be explored would be through an international design competition. The results of their call for conceptual design using ColorCore succeeded beyond their wildest dreams. The eleven winners and ten invited celebrity architects of their "Surface and Ornament" competition tested the product to its limits, creating functional art that demonstrated ColorCore's translucency, its ability to be routed, layered, inlaid, and bent. Not only did the display inspire a traveling museum exhibit ("Material Evidence: New Color Techniques in Handmade Furniture"), it also went a long way toward helping establish the High Touch aesthetic as a trend in design and not merely an editorial conceit.

Who Designs High Touch?

We have two stereotypes about designers and neither one is entirely wrong. One comes courtesy of Ayn Rand's *The Fountainhead* and the powerful personalities of Frank Lloyd Wright, Ludwig Mies van der Rohe, and Le Corbusier: the designer as all-powerful, far-seeing, and wise. We're cynical; we can afford to let go of that one. But the other is dearer to our hearts: the struggling young artist whose vision is pure, who triumphs over economic adversity by using found objects and inexpensive, easily accessible building materials to realize his or her vision.

Some High Touch designs do have the outward appearance of having been slung together by a ten-year-old with an unfortunate propensity for robbing building sites, but, in fact, High Touch has a sophistication born of design-school training and experience in physical craftsmanship. In "distressing" concrete pillars to make the legs of a table, one must know how much can be safely bashed off and tossed away. In using a pool-ladder metaphor in seating, a great sense of proportion is required. Making a table with a sturdy base of yardsticks and a perfectly hexagonal yardstick-rimmed top only looks simple.

The people who design High Touch objects differ in geographic locales, backgrounds, and professional employ. They include some struggling artists and established luminaries, as well as industrial designers working on a royalty basis and interior designers and architects who design products as a sideline. Disconcertingly, they can be the same people who design Modernist objects. One has to look beyond the who and the immediate why to *what* causes High Touch. There is a strong connection to the crafts revolution of the early 1970s. Both rebel against the streamlining of furniture during our Machine Age and International Style periods, when handcrafts got lost in the rush to conquer the machine.

The effect of all these streamlined products—not only furniture, but radios, clocks, cars, telephones, and refrigerators—was enough to inspire a number of antiestablishment dropouts of the late 1960s to become the craftworkers of the next decade, initiating courses in practical design and manufacture of furniture, jewelry and ceramics as well as fine art.

Their furniture designs use the interplay between practicality and art, and draw on a broad field of styles and concepts, but the designers have one thing in common. They began designing and making furniture because they couldn't find what they wanted in retail furniture stores. A large percentage of High Touch designers has worked with their materials by hand.

For High Touch designers, the process of making an object is essential to understanding it. Their work will often let the materials speak for themselves in raw, unprocessed forms, creating a "living" object that responds to heat, moisture, and the environment. A designer of concrete chairs once poured concrete at construction sites. One designer, whose father was an industrial designer, explores new materials as they are developed and become available. Another furniture designer was a sculptor first, and specifies steel in her seating because she thoroughly understands how it must be worked.

The furniture and objects in this book tend to be one-of-a-kind and custom-order works. In fact, very little was designed specifically for mass production. Ron Rezek and Brian Kane are professional designers who know how to adapt a design for production technology. Charles Pfister designs buildings, their interiors, and the accessories that accent those interiors.

The high end of the furniture industry, the part that sells only to architects and interior designers, has approached several craft-oriented makers of one-of-a-kind pieces. Elizabeth Browning Jackson, for example, is working on a chair with Arc International.

The doors are not so quickly slammed against conceptual furniture designers as they once were, but some still need to produce their own designs just to get them on the market. Arc International was formed by a designer, Joe Duke, who turned to small woodworking shops to execute his designs. Arc now takes over the preproduction development of handmade limited-edition furniture for select artists and ensures that the cost is spread out over a production run. This helps to keep the pieces economically feasible.

ABOVE: A concrete stool, designed by Hermann Becker of Krefeld, West Germany, has a raw, yet honest quality. The seat is covered in industrial felt, for a bit of restrained warmth.

In New York City, there are tiny showroom galleries in widely divergent neighborhoods, from funky Soho to the established design center. Gratifyingly, their customers are just as diverse a crowd. "We see doctors and lawyers who come in to look and can't leave without an item. They don't know why they like it, but they have to own it," said Ivy Ross, a partner in the Clodagh, Ross and Williams gallery. The high profile Gallery of Applied Art, which acts as a showroom for Arc, attracts collectors as well. Furniture Club works to specification with designers and architects and people who walk in off the street. It's safe to surmise that every major city in America has designer-manufacturers and tiny galleries where High Touch is sold at prices ranging from $35 for papier-mâché sunglasses to $13,000 for large-scale furniture.

2

SEATING

ave a seat.

There is a world of diversity in that simple invitation. Since 1950, seating has been made from fiberglass, pressure-molded polyester, fabric stretched between steel rods, plastic, polyfoam—the litany of materials sounds like a chemical supply catalogue. In exploring the properties of each new material, the design community abandoned traditional form for the conceptual, and chairs have been plastic-shelled "eggs," polyfoam Marilyn lips, pellet-filled leather bags, fiberglass buckets, and leather slings.

Obviously, exploration of materials in High Touch seating has precedents. But the use of old and new materials in aggressively nontraditional ways and the forms they take in High Touch have resulted in changing our idea of what a chair should be. It is in seating that High Touch is applied the most prolifically and at times, the most inventively.

LEFT: Robert Robinson, a designer from Chicago, covered a wooden chair design with worn barn tin for a High Touch statement. BELOW: Jack Larimore's *Chair's Chair* combines ColorCore, curly maple, Honduras mahogany, ebony, leather, lacquer paint, gilding, silk ribbon, and electrical components to create a statement that speaks not only of materials, but of the power of a chair.

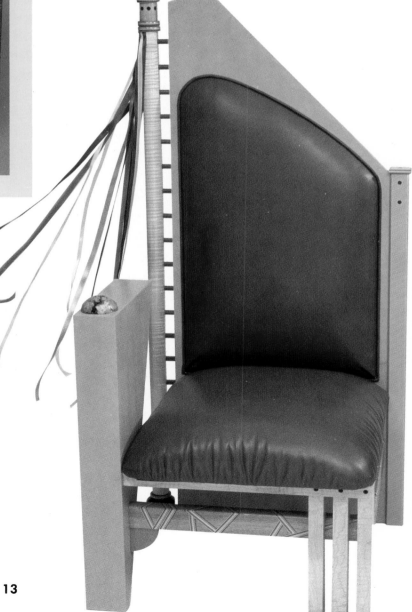

We take it for granted that the purpose of seating is to provide a place to sit down. William H. Whyte put it neatly when he said, "Seating is a prosthesis for feet." But seating is not just a place to sit. There are two distinct types of seating products: the functional and the ceremonial. Usually what is ceremonial retains some function, and vice versa. Those who design the functional chairs, benches, sofas, chaise lounges, and

PAGE 11: ColorCore solid-color laminate, plywood, white oak, wenge, and Baltic birch are combined in Michael Pierschalla's *Pair of Chairs.* The Cambridge, Massachusetts, woodworker has incorporated a new material into his primarily wood-oriented vocabulary. LEFT: Chicago architect Stanley Tigerman, asked to use ColorCore in a Formica promotion, tested the material's ability to bend in his pastel-striped *Tête-à-Tête.*

stools attempt first to meet specific seating needs, putting engineering, comfort, and probable use before aesthetics. The ergonomic seating that revolutionized office seating is a benefit of research done by the FAA for its air traffic controllers, and by the automobile industry for car drivers and passengers.

The choice of materials in function-oriented seating is dictated by the characteristics a material can offer to make the seat more comfortable, more practical, or more durable. For instance, airport seating is often made of plastic not because it provides nominal seating comfort for a limited amount of time, but because the properties of plastic make it durable, mass-produceable, and relatively vandal-proof. The leavening in this too-practical mix is color; plastic can be imbued with color of unusual intensities and hues, and this, with the sculptural shapes of plastic seating, can make airport waiting more bearable.

Making a statement is the primary concern of ceremonial seating. Thrones are large and imposing; stools indicate the lower status of their occupants. In a high tech room filled with computers and other electronic gadgetry, the seating can be a traditional Chippendale chair—a ceremonial application. The chair offers emotional comfort, a historical reference, and reassures the sitter of his place in the world.

ABOVE: The *Concrete Chair,* by David Hertz of Los Angeles, is constructed from a specially developed lightweight cement, which allows for its simple sculptural form, reminiscent in spirit to the curvilinear wooden designs by Finnish architect Alvar Aalto. Hertz was inspired to use the material when pouring foundation slabs on construction sites during his architecture-school days.

Ceremonial seating reflects individual tastes, as well as ideas of comfort, both physical and psychological. The lines of demarcation between ceremonial and functional blur when the chair's entire function is ceremony. Mies van der Rohe's *Barcelona* chair was designed in 1929 as an elegant prop, a two-of-a-kind sculpture in white leather to represent seating for a royal party during a presentation. The functional purpose of the infinitely elegant pedestal-based tulip chairs of Eero Saarinen (1956) was to "clear up the slum of legs . . . to make the chair all one thing again," yet this chair fulfills a ceremonial statement of modern good taste. The base is cast alloy with plastic coating, the seats are pressure-molded white polyester with fabric-covered padding, and the shape is less geometric than organic.

Thus, ceremonial seating carries a message, either

E

F

of reassurance or status or something more symbolic. Among the reassuring designs are one-of-a-kinds where the furniture-maker may be called a conceptual artist. The beauty, craftsmanship, and cleverness of these unusual pieces are admired more than their utility or the possibility for mass production.

High Touch chairs fall into the ceremonial category more often than not. Some High Touch seating is only the symbol of a chair. Object becomes icon, and the

BOTH PAGES: Seating designs by Milan's Zeus group share a taste for the minimal, but incorporate High Touch materials. The *Lubecca Poltroncina* (A), designed by Maurizio Peregalli, has a formed rubber seat and back. Many of Peregalli's designs use Pirelli 1000-point rubber floor-matting as the cushion surface, including the *Sgabello Altro Cromo* (B), the *Savonarola* (C), the *Poltroncina* (D), the *Sedia Cromo* (E), the *Panca* (F), and the *Sgabello Basso Cromo* (G). Davide Mercatali and Paolo Pedrizetti have put a flexible rubber seat and back in their *Tarzan* chair (H).

H

G

LEFT: *Snowflake,* a furniture series consisting of a large low table and six matching chairs—in an almost Japanese manner—is constructed of galvanized metal channel, a material that is generally used in conjunction with metal two-by-fours to construct fireproof building walls. The galvanizing process involves a coating of zinc that creates a crystalline surface effect on the basically raw metal. The pattern, according to furniture-maker Paul Ludick of New York City, is similar in appearance to frost on a window, which inspired the piece's title. Chair backs are covered in Neoprene rubber.

observation of function is only one of the guidelines the High Touch designer follows in creating seating. The message is important.

Tradition, culture, and use have formed our concepts of what a chair ought to be. The High Touch designer manipulates this concept, reduces it to its sculptural equivalent, and seeks out new materials. The results can change the way we perceive chairs.

Consider the Bauhaus tubular steel-frame chairs. Despite the insistence of their designers that the chairs were made for mass production and to explore a Machine Age ideal, the new forms were startling. They lacked conventional springs, cushions, and boxy wooden frames; they lacked a conventional reference.

ABOVE: Steven Holl and Tucker Viemeister of New York City employ elements associated with the backyard, suburban plunge in their *Pool Chair.* Tile and a metal pool ladder combined with a blue-tinted Plexiglas seat complete the referential picture.

LEFT: Paul Ludick's *Apartheid Chair,* with its chain-link fence seat back, has obvious political meaning. The wooden frame of the chair is purposely house-shaped and the multicolored paint pattern is representative of a mix of races. Note that the back panel at the rear of the chair is without the painted pattern, a subtle reference to segregation.

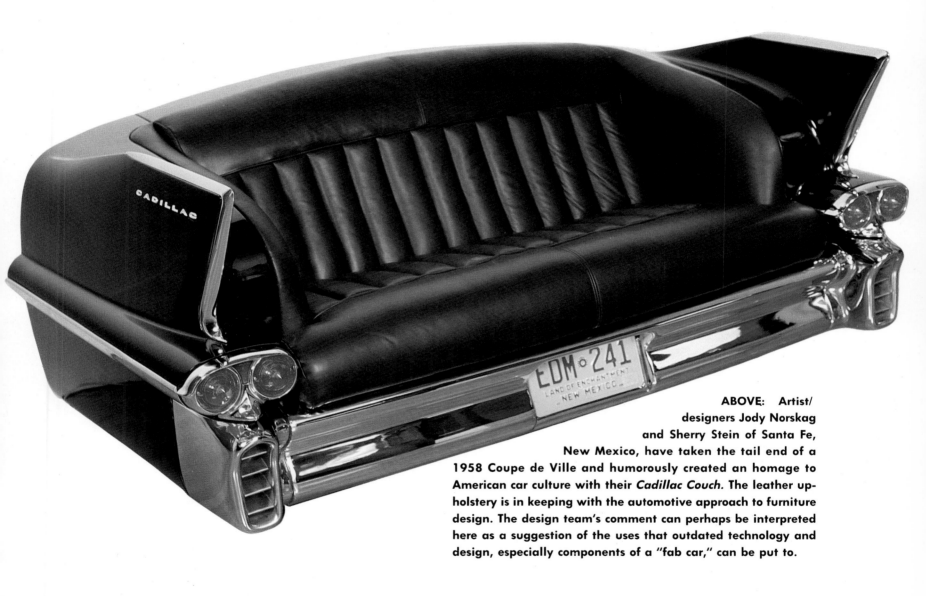

ABOVE: Artist/
designers Jody Norskag
and Sherry Stein of Santa Fe,
New Mexico, have taken the tail end of a
1958 Coupe de Ville and humorously created an homage to
American car culture with their *Cadillac Couch.* The leather upholstery is in keeping with the automotive approach to furniture
design. The design team's comment can perhaps be interpreted
here as a suggestion of the uses that outdated technology and
design, especially components of a "fab car," can be put to.

They are successful now, more than fifty years after they were designed, but this cutting-edge design was a commercial failure in its infancy.

Marcel Breuer's *Wassily* chair is more about his particular vision of design than it is about providing a comfortable place to sit: "I was thinking about replacing the thick upholstery used on chair seats by stretched fabric. The combination of stretchable fabric and a flexible frame I hoped would make the chair more comfortable to sit in and keep it from looking

LEFT: The elegantly minimal *Day Bed* designed by Maurizio Peregalli and Sergio Calatroni as part of the Zeus Collection of Milan combines metal, wood, and rubber for a distinctly materials-oriented design. While the pillows of wood are statements of geometry rather than inviting places to lay your head, the rubber matting, used as the sleeping or seating surface, replaces both foam cushioning and upholstery with one fell swoop, yet does not interfere with the simple, linear silhouette that the designers envisioned.

LEFT: This steel side chair by designer/artist Forrest Myers of New York City has a light-reactive and colorful presence thanks to Myers' sanding the metal surface in a swirling pattern and dyeing the entire piece. The chair is as simple in construction as it looks, allowing the material to speak for itself without interruption. Myers also uses aluminum for many of his designs, using the same techniques with that material.
RIGHT: Swedish furniture designer Jonas Bohlin has designed a concrete chair, adopting concrete slabs for use as the seat, back, and support in the same way that a more conventional designer might use wood. The straight-backed, rather rigid placement of the slabs in relation to one another, combined with the unfinished steel arms and legs offer an undoubtably cold aesthetic; but with age and the "natural" effects of moisture, staining and even cracking, the chair might "warm up."

clumsy. In the course of my work on series manufacture and standardization I had come across the polished metal surface—reflecting, pure lines in space—as new components of our home furnishings. In these shimmering, curving lines I saw not only symbols of modern technology but technology itself."

He wanted to work with the tubular steel. Of that he was certain, but he only *hoped* it would make the chair more comfortable.

High Touch seating designers also are guilty of considering the material first and the comfort of the user second. The designs fall into two camps: one

where nontraditional materials are used as a practical alternative to conventional construction, and the other wherein imagery is the foremost concern and materials are chosen to support the artist/designer's vision.

Using nontraditional materials, the designers in Milan's Zeus group give the user a fresh sensory experience by substituting rubber for conventional fabric-covered cushions. Plastic laminates and plastic surfacing materials applied to a sitting surface retain all the practical aspects that suited them to counter-top use, but they can be manipulated, colored, and composed into startling designs. Stanley Tigerman's almost

ABOVE: Rubber is used to sheath metal legs and provide a flexible sitter-reactive back support in San Francisco-based designer Brian Kane's *Rubber Chair* produced by the Metropolitan Furniture Company. The soft, tactile surface of the rubber frame contrasts with the hard surface of the maplewood seat. An added characteristic of the rubber-covered legs is that, unlike metal legs, when these come into contact with the legs of other pieces of furniture such as tables or desks, they do not scratch other surfaces. Kane has used rubber to achieve a look and feel for his chair that is unique and practical.

ABOVE: Visions of surfboards, 1950s automobile fins, hot-red metal-flake finishes, and the living room furniture found in cartoon icon George Jetson's space-age abode are combined in *Gloria,* a distinctly wild and personal statement by its designer, Elizabeth Browning Jackson of New York City. Though full of period references, the technology of making the bench is pure High Touch, as are its materials. Adapting the fiberglass molding process used for decades by surfboard manufacturers, Jackson has applied it to furnishings design. And, of course, one must consider that despite its rather garish presence, it is practical for people with children. Like the hull of a ship or a surfer's stick, it is completely water-resistant.

anthropomorphic ColorCore loveseat, *Tête-à-Tête,* has striped curves and a sinuous grace that invites use, but the surface is completely unyielding. The piece demands that the sitter conform to the seat—just the opposite effect of the last decade's bean bag chairs that conform to the sitter. Tigerman's piece says look, touch, but don't sit for long.

High Touch seating designers pluck materials from industries unrelated to furniture design to imbue the concept of seating with new meaning. Take Elizabeth Browning Jackson's fiberglass *Gloria* sofa into the water and you have a quasi surfboard. Found objects are employed in chair design, creating a Pop Art portrait of a common image as in a sofa by Norskag and Stein, where the tail end of a 1958 Cadillac becomes the structure. Automobile parts, household objects, recycled building materials, and other "inventions" are used to jar our perceptions of what is acceptable, to appeal to our emotions, to expand the meanings of common forms and surfaces.

In exploring new forms, High Touch innovators follow the tradition of Alvar Aalto and Charles Eames, whose molding experiments with wood not only gave us forms that are sensuously curvilinear, but expanded the known uses of wood in furniture design. Concrete and raw steel, the vocabulary of construction sites, can be molded or bent into rather poetic shapes, as in David Hertz' *Concrete Chair* or Forrest Myers' *Steel Chair*, both striking in appearance and well-removed from their conventional contexts. Myers' *Steel Chair* speaks to a plastic aesthetic, demanding appreciation of material over form as it proclaims its dominance— by virtue of superior durability—over plastic and fiberglass-reinforced plastic. The poetry in Hertz' poured and molded chair lies in what is *not* there. Its spaces are as important to its design integrity as is its solidity. Both are occasional rather than "easy" chairs.

High Touch seating can also have a handmade craft/artisan appearance, as in Robert Robinson's *Barn Tin Chair* or Paul Ludick's chain-link backed *Apartheid Chair*. Michael Pierschalla uses ColorCore curves for his high-backed *Pair of Chairs*. The curves indicate the boundaries of the seat, act as support on one side only, and provide whimsical visual balance as a symbolic

chair arm in this otherwise angular composition. These unique designs have a dynamic sensory dimension and a thought-provoking symbolism that puts them into the furniture-as-sculpture category.

A Patrick Naggar upholstered wing chair redefines the term in its eccentric construction. Instead of an interior frame that is not only hidden but whose shape can be masked by cushions and upholstery, Naggar gives us an ebonized-wood external frame with etched plexiglass wings. The cushioned back and seat is a concession to convention and comfort. The chair's dimensions reflect Naggar's Egyptian heritage in that its legs are shorter and broader than is customary this side of the Suez Canal, and the depth of the seat recalls early Chinese seating.

Sometimes comfort seems irrelevant to High Touch designers. The seating surfaces are often too flat and unyielding and the "fabric" of the seat is hostile, as when cement, tin, laminates, and glass are used. The plexiglass seat in Holl and Viemeister's *Pool Chair* does curve slightly, but only to suggest rippling water. The rubber flooring often used in High Touch for chair seats and backs is hedonistically flexible by comparison; the *Cadillac Couch* by Norskag and Stein offers a luxuriously soft seat.

Little of the seating shown in this chapter is mass-produced. The notable exceptions are chairs from Brian Kane and Milan's Zeus group, which is made up of Maurizio Peregalli, Davide Peregalli, and Paolo Pedrizetti. This does not mean that High Touch is completely incompatible with mass production, or that designing for limited mass production prevents an artist from creating a chair with a message. Patrick Naggar's work, for example is produced in limited editions by Arc International.

3
TABLES

We do not ask that a table do much more than provide a flat surface for writing, dining, or holding objects. Depending on its probable use, the table must be of a certain height, width, or circumference. Its appearance reflects the tastes and choices of both owner and designer. One person might prefer a wooden table with a highly polished surface or an oiled finish that requires constant care. Someone else might want a table with a distressed, timeworn surface whose patina reflects the history of the piece and lends an appreciable warmth. With steel and glass, one cannot disassociate the materials from their use in the Bauhaus and Modernist design movements.

The table may be the simplest of all design problems with which the High Touch designer must contend, because tables have only the one flat surface that need be strictly functional. The construction and composition of the base affords ample room for invention. Materials can be borrowed from almost any context and used to support that easiest of all solutions, the plate-glass top. Consequently, we see concrete forms, aluminum, found objects, and just about anything at all being employed as a table base. A corrugated cardboard carton might just as easily support a table top as a pile of bricks.

This kind of table does not really challenge the material but it does attack our concept of what a table can and should look like. Using new materials or old materials in a new way adds novelty, texture, and humor to a design composition. They elevate seemingly

PAGE 29: This table designed by Carl Tese of New York explores the potential for patterning the surface of concrete for an unusual textural effect. LEFT, OPPOSITE: Furniture designer Terence Main of New York combines a rough concrete base with a decorated etched-glass top in this cocktail-table design. RIGHT: The *K1004 Moiré Table/Desk,* designed by Bruce Keiser and Don Newman of Philadelphia, has an anodized aluminum frame and a simple glass top. What is notable about the piece is the layer of nylon mesh that the designers have placed under the glass surface. The mesh, normally used in industrial situations, is layered and, to the viewer's eye, creates a moiré effect. Keiser and Newman prefer not to use anodized aluminum as the primary table surface, citing that it is not scratch-resistant or especially durable. Most of their tables feature clear glass tops.

BELOW: The table top of the *Nugo Table,* designed by Michael Walsh of Boston, makes a materials statement with the combination of three treatments of granite. Black rubber wheels complete the elegant assemblage. **NEAR RIGHT, OPPOSITE:** Carlton Cook, a designer from Houston, might just be the "king" of materials adaptive re-use. His *Gross Table* employs bowling balls, Corian, rubber hose, marbles, and stainless steel. Cook obviously combs the junkyards of urban Texas to find a suitable range of design supplies. **TOP RIGHT, OPPOSITE:** Chicago interior designer and furniture-maker John Cockrell often makes custom furnishings for his residential and commercial projects. His *Corian Table,* designed for a joint *Interiors* magazine/Dupont project, explores the potential for using Corian in the same way as wood. Cockrell has jigsawed the material into a free-form design and has used it as the supporting element of the glass-topped table. Spiky aluminum legs and sculptural caps are also included. **BOTTOM LEFT, OPPOSITE:** French designer Patrick Naggar's *Knossos Table* features a leg detail made of terra cotta clay.

unsuitable or unusable materials to essential elements. Los Angeles-based designer David Hertz uses concrete in this way, as does New York-based Terence Main, who adds textural interest to the glass surface. Philadelphia's Keiser/Newman team places an aluminum screen under the glass top to create a visually exciting light-interactive moiré effect. The clash of smooth, cool glass and rough, organic rock shapes addresses the new Stone Age in a table by Bonetti/Garouste.

A more daring approach replaces wood or glass as the functional table surface. A designer may stretch the viewer's sense of what is beautiful by elevating a material such as plastic laminate, with its dinette association, or aluminum, with its backyard furniture

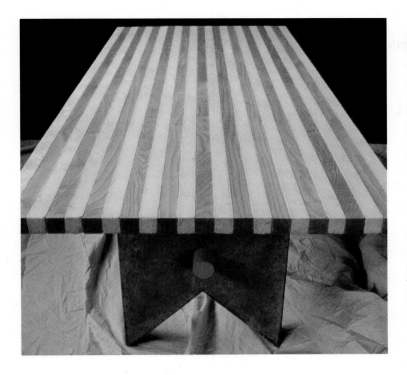

practicality, into the realm of being appreciated for its innate and often unexplored characteristics. Jay Adams' *Mesa Table*, for instance, uses Corian as a surface, but exploits its ability to be worked like wood by adding tiny Plexiglas inlays that allow light to pass through. Michael Walsh has managed to create refined table designs from plastic laminates because of the way he uses them for table tops.

A new vision and appreciation of materials evolves when one pits Corian against the glow of wood or the texture of concrete against smooth, cool glass. We can look beyond stereotypes and enliven our environments with varied surface treatments. These materials develop their own patinas of use and time, and appeal to the human need for change and visual stimulation. A simple Parsons-style table by Furniture Club, with a top of dyed concrete, might even crack at the edges over a period of time and with use.

LEFT, OPPOSITE: The *K1000* table, designed and manufactured in Philadelphia by Bruce Keiser and Don Newman, has a pedestal base made of anodized aluminum and a ribbed porcelain element. The porcelain process is most commonly used in the manufacture of high-strength industrial componentry. The layered-glass table top can be lit from inside the base, creating a luminous effect. **ABOVE:** Alternating strips of yellow-dyed ash wood and blue-dyed concrete form the top of the *Piper* dining table, designed by Jay Adams. Base pieces are gray concrete connected by a pink wooden tube.

LEFT, OPPOSITE: Bruce Tomb and John Randolph of San Francisco mixed concrete with aggregate and iron oxide pigments to make the rough-edged supports for this table. The table top, supported by a steel structure, has an unpolished and sandblasted glass top that completes the primitive look.

ABOVE: The *Pina Gamba* console table, designed by Myra and Geoffrey Frost of Topanga, California, features an etched-glass top "floating" on black Neoprene-rubber bumpers set in the kind of roughly textured concrete columns usually reserved for parking lots or roadside bollards.

There is a preponderance of designers using concrete for High Touch table design. Like plastic, concrete has both fluid and solid properties, and can be dyed. It is considerably heavier than plastic, which may explain why concrete seating has been limited to theme parks, and why concrete did not become the design craze of the late 1960s as plastic did. It is easily available in premixed formulations. Chips of almost any solid—glass, marble, agate, metal filings—can be added to concrete for visual and textural effect. Once set, the molded material is rigid and can be sculpted to refine or roughen the shaping. The surface texture can take on the graining of plywood, be glass-smooth as in terrazzo, lightly pebbled with acrylic coatings to prevent staining, or slightly rough and chalky as it appears in its natural state.

Furniture Club's Don Ruddy and Shane Kennedy were attracted to concrete's fluidity and mold-ability. The two protected their living-room floor with plastic sheeting and began experimenting with dyes and forms, eventually settling on a modular block approach to table design. The modules allow the table to be taken apart for easier moving, and give interior designer and architect clients the flexibility to specify different colors and textures within a single piece of furniture.

The concrete aficionados favor simple shapes, such as spheres, cubes, pyramids, and many of the table designs have a mathematical purity that the barest of bare-box minimalists would appreciate. Most often, the concrete forms the base and the table top material is chosen merely to enhance; however, concrete tops are not unheard of and can be very effective.

When furniture design is looked at as fine art, it is in table design that we find the most blatantly artistic examples. Rex Designs' concrete tables feature painterly, modeled surfaces applied to geometric forms. Carlton Cook's bowling ball, Corian, and rubber assemblages are like collages: you must look at the total effect and not the pieces to appreciate them.

Patrick Naggar does nothing to challenge one's idea of a "table," but his interplay of materials imbues each table with a story. There is a quality of danger and brooding in his *Knossos Table,* as if it looms in the background to metamorphose into a mythical monster.

The Corian pin-dots set regularly into the ColorCore top suggest reptilian scales, and the bits of ribbon solidly tacked at intervals around the wooden rim become the tattered clothing of an opponent long gone. The beehive terra cotta leg detail, positioned where leg meets table top, seem to simulate leg joints. The piece is not only rich in texture and use of materials, but in the evocations and imagery it produces. Although it is clearly a work of art, this table can be made to order.

Wendall Castle is a furniture craftsman who can

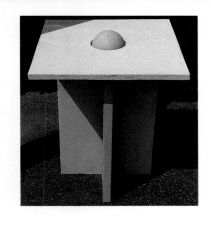

not be considered a High Touch designer but who did create one truly High Touch design worthy of note, if only as an excellent example of what is being done with diverse materials in table design. For "Material Evidence," the collaborative exhibition of the Gallery at Workbench, the Formica Corporation, and the Smithsonian Institution, he fash-

ioned a physical pun, a *Coffee Table* whose usable surface is so small it holds a single cup. The cherry table top is a square pyramid rising to a fixed ceramic saucer (the cup is separate and usable). The four legs are prevented from seeming overgrown and overblown by curving striped bands of inlaid ColorCore, which draw the eye upward like the rims of so many bubbles.

When color is important to design integrity, plastic laminates are invaluable to the table designer. Offered

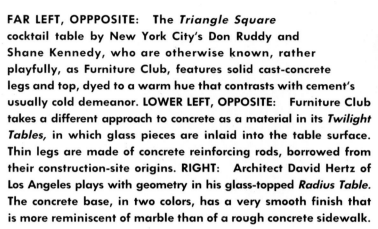

FAR LEFT, OPPPOSITE: The *Triangle Square* cocktail table by New York City's Don Ruddy and Shane Kennedy, who are otherwise known, rather playfully, as Furniture Club, features solid cast-concrete legs and top, dyed to a warm hue that contrasts with cement's usually cold demeanor. **LOWER LEFT, OPPOSITE:** Furniture Club takes a different approach to concrete as a material in its *Twilight Tables,* in which glass pieces are inlaid into the table surface. Thin legs are made of concrete reinforcing rods, borrowed from their construction-site origins. **RIGHT:** Architect David Hertz of Los Angeles plays with geometry in his glass-topped *Radius Table.* The concrete base, in two colors, has a very smooth finish that is more reminiscent of marble than of a rough concrete sidewalk.

in 300 high-gloss and matte colors and textures ranging from smooth to lightly pebbled to *faux* slate, plastic laminates are manufactured by several companies and thus are accessible to the designer. Formica's second-generation plastic surfacing, ColorCore, comes in ninety colors. Its palette and the fact that it cold-forms into curves without snapping has inspired polychrome table tops whose surfacing material is pieced into intricate designs like elaborate marquetry, the woodworking technique of the last century.

The combination of glass and metal has spelled "contemporary" to consumers for the last thirty years, to the point where it seemed that nothing new could be done with it. One expects highly polished chrome, steel, or aluminum to be paired with glass for residential use, and brushed metals to be paired with exotic woods or plastic laminates and chipboard for office

and institutional use. It is this conditioned expectation of a design cliché that makes new uses so refreshing. Paul Ludick's galvanized metal with its crystalline surface detail as shown in *Snowflake*, and Forrest Myers' color-anodized aluminum are welcome diversions. The plastic laminate surface of Ron Rezek's *Squiggle* desk and dining table rests on side panels of corrugated aluminum. Patinated sheet steel is the top for *Wintour*, a *soigné* dining table with sandblasted, ebonized mahogany legs. The shape is Modernist geometry but the play of texture and color is pure High Touch. Designed by Alan Buchsbaum, it is manufactured by Ecart and available through Furniture of the Twentieth Century. Forrest Myers' 41-inch, three-legged foyer table topped with glass is a structural anomaly, for the weight of the glass top supports the legs.

Where High Touch ends and functional art begins

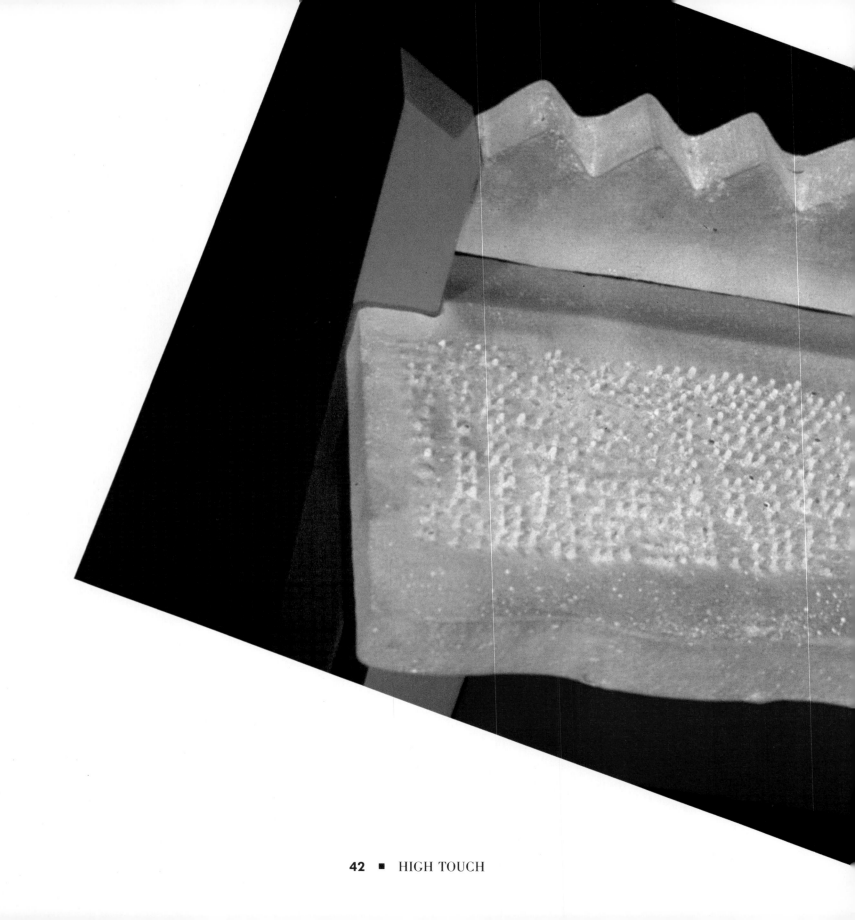

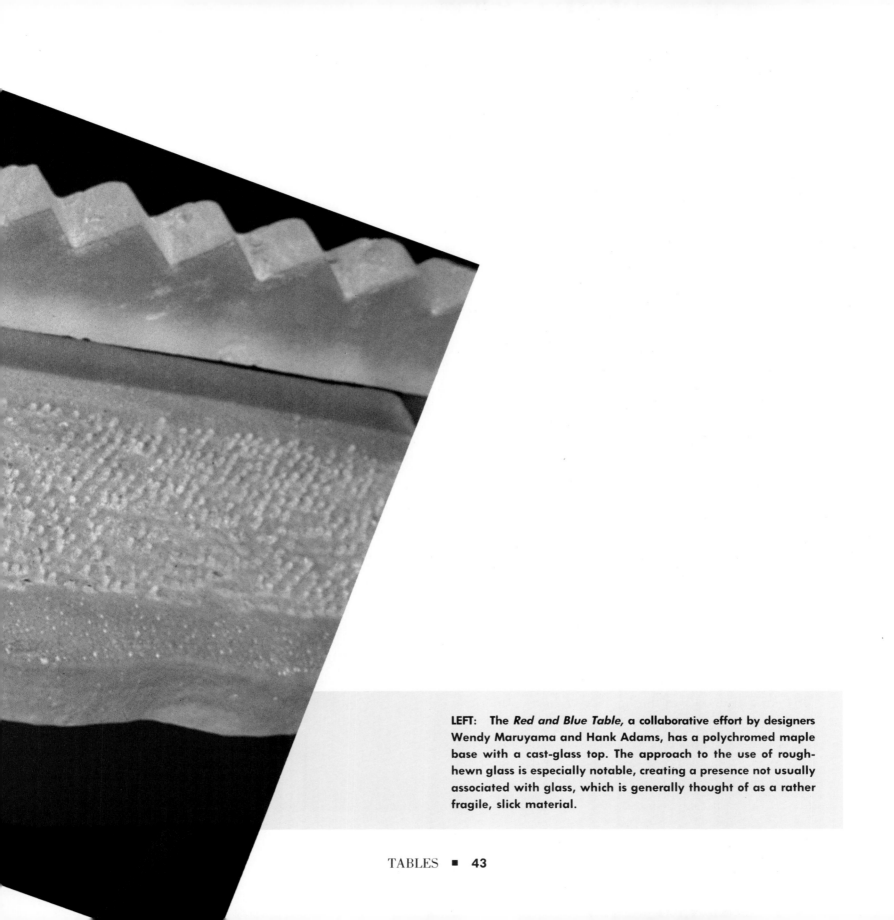

LEFT: The *Red and Blue Table,* a collaborative effort by designers Wendy Maruyama and Hank Adams, has a polychromed maple base with a cast-glass top. The approach to the use of rough-hewn glass is especially notable, creating a presence not usually associated with glass, which is generally thought of as a rather fragile, slick material.

is a moot point, a distinction best left to the individual artists. Richard Helzer's *Neolithic Charting Table* combines lead, bronze, cast aluminum, wood, Formica laminate, and stone in a manner that accents the textural differences while telling a story. The 16″ x 22″ x 22″ piece is part of a traveling exhibition entitled "Form Beyond Function: Recent Sculpture by North American Metalsmiths," co-sponsored by the Mitchell Museum (Illinois) and the Society of North American Metalsmiths. In the pattern of many High Touch artists, Helzer and forty other metalsmiths ignore function to probe beyond the conventional boundaries of the craft tradition, and technique is of subsidiary importance to design expression.

LEFT, OPPOSITE PAGE: Adopting one of the most common household objects, the yardstick, furniture-maker John Marcoux has elevated it beyond its original purpose, making one appreciate its quirky pattern. His *One Yard Table* is a clever and complicated assemblage involving not only sticks, but steel and bronze glass as well for a combined-materials effort.

ABOVE: Exploring the potential of dyeing concrete in various unorthodox colors, designer/architect Jay Adams, who calls his San Francisco firm Bow Wow House, has created *Boxer*, a series of end tables. The rich texture of the concrete is not eliminated in the dyeing process. The table tops are aluminum.

STORAGE

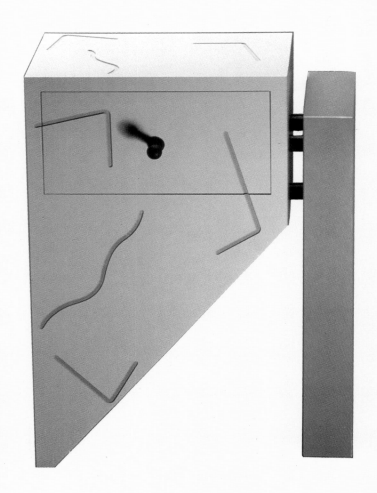

High Touch storage requires a leap of faith on the part of its user. It is not a system of stackable units that blend into any decor, but individual sculptures with functional attributes. For example, Jonas Bohlin's angular magazine rack zigzags toward the ceiling and has function beyond mere containment of artifacts. Magazines placed against its angles become a colorful display, and the limited display space reminds us that not only are magazines disposable cul-

ture, they *should* be disposed of in time.

With the possible exception of industrial metal shelving, no storage piece is simply functional. The austerity of storage pieces by Modernist design leaders Florence Knoll, Charles Eames, George Nelson, and Joe Colombo reflects the social mores of the 1950s and 1960s. Just as one's frustrations and passions were to be hidden behind a polite mask, so was the detritus of living to be concealed and contained behind doors

and in drawers. The 1950s pieces had the unintentional whimsy of foot-high wire or wooden legs that made them easy to clean under, but later storage ran floor to ceiling, presenting blank facades of the designer's material of choice, often oiled teak or laminate-covered wood. The beauty of the surface was supposed to be an adequate replacement for lush carvings and other surface decoration. It is this belief that every inch of space must be accounted for, that space is wasted unless it can contain and conceal, that designers of High Touch storage pieces react against. High Touch designers cheerfully waste space, sacrificing the volume of containment to offer visual gratification in stacked angles, pediments, and imaginatively stylized anthropomorphism.

Yet there is a dilemma in modern life. Our love of novelty commands that we acquire things, but the cost of space makes it hard to keep them. For the pack rat, nothing less than the highly functional industrial solution of myriads of sizes of drawers and bins will suffice. And those who live surrounded by their objects in the cheerful clutter of the English Country look have already found their solutions.

For the rest of us, the answer must lie elsewhere. We have on the one hand a vast population trying to impose order on the chaos of artifacts in their homes, and on the other an architectural elite that advocates controlling clutter by carting it all to the nearest dump. The high tech design movement offered one solution, saying that using rescued gym lockers is a design statement, that industrial steel shelving is a design statement, that camp beds used as guest accommodations is not, in fact, stingy and inhospitable, but a statement of a minimalist design ethic. What it is, finally, is an admission that clutter has won.

PRECEDING PAGE: The *Smallboy,* a one-drawer chest by Wendy Maruyama, is made of ColorCore, routed to produce a two-color patterned surface, plywood and lacquer. Drawer-pull is made of rubber. **LEFT, OPPOSITE:** Writing desk by Ron Christensen has practical as well as playful concerns. Although made of concrete with the intention of recalling building sections, the desk's writing area is leather covered to provide a smooth, luxe surface. Aircraft warning lights and steel I-beam supports contribute to the overall architectural effect. Graffitied "wall" is a send-up on the piece's function—after all, a desk is to "write" on. **ABOVE:** Bookcase by Furniture Club has a concrete base, metal support, and routed, patterned Corian shelves.

Such statements lose their impact after a while, and it is necessary to seek new answers to the problem of organizing one's personal effects. The closet organizers and modular storage units currently at retail are less designed than engineered, and they very carefully reflect no particular style, the better to blend into many different backgrounds.

Something has to step away from the background; everything cannot be background. High Touch addresses this problem.

Ron Christensen's concrete *Graffiti Desk* probably takes up more room than a Chippendale secretary, but its presence is a dramatic statement. Dennis Higgins' patinated and painted bronze magazine rack is more sculptural than functional, but it does take a few magazines from the pile growing on the carpet.

Wendy Maruyama's *Smallboy* chest, a rectangle with a triangular bite removed, reminds us that even contemporary furniture does not have to be merely functional. Maruyama has layered ColorCore and grouted it in places to reveal the second color so that shape and surface decoration reenter into the vocabulary of contemporary design.

High Touch designers have expanded textural vocabulary by dabbling in the absurd. Fantasy, imagery, and allusion, which had been streamlined out of existence, are on the rise, thanks to a reactionary interest in shape and materials.

Stephen Whittlesey salvages old boards from derelict buildings and rotted piers and works them into furniture the way a painter composes a canvas. The pieces are easily recognizable as dressers or cupboards and they offer visual referents to bygone architectural excesses. A pediment, a molding, a bit of Victorian "gingerbread" trim, and other emotionally satisfying

LEFT, OPPOSITE: Standing magazine rack by Swedish designer Jonas Bohlin has a concrete base for a reason. It provides a weighty base to support the zig-zagged Cherrywood shelves. The structure is, as is often the case in High Touch storage designs, more geared to sculptural effect than function. **RIGHT:** Magazine rack by Dennis Higgins is made of cast bronze with applied, primary-colored patinas. Higgins makes bronze a more playful material with jagged-edge details, cut-outs, and unlikely color selections, changing the historic perception of the material.

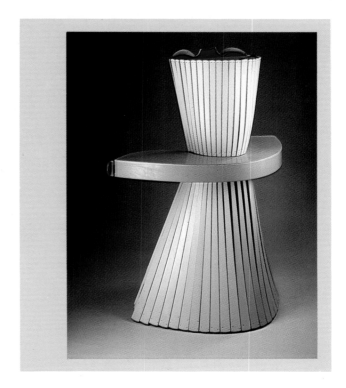

Dress Her/Liquor Cabinet by Jay Stanger is functional as well as symbolic, and is, of course, made of a High Touch material: ColorCore laminate with beefwood and plywood. The cabinet is designed in the image of a prom dress. The wit of the piece is inherent in the functioning aspects of the various doors Stanger has made. The "dress" has a drop front and a "skirt" that opens widely and freely. To create the pleated back of the cabinet, ColorCore strips are placed side-by-side in a fan pattern.

ABOVE: Featuring somewhat anthropomorphic forms, the *Kitchen Friend*, a storage unit designed by the Los Angeles design team Niemi Klein Millar, also known as A2Z, is made of Formica-covered wood and steel.

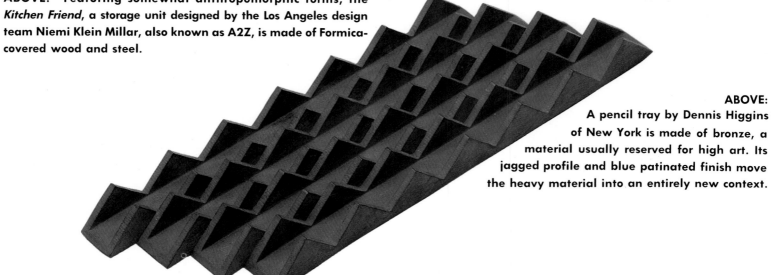

ABOVE:
A pencil tray by Dennis Higgins of New York is made of bronze, a material usually reserved for high art. Its jagged profile and blue patinated finish move the heavy material into an entirely new context.

BELOW: The concept of architectonic furniture is again addressed by Atlanta designer Ron Christensen in this imposing chest made of oak, concrete, and fabric. In a sense, storage is about covering up, so why not enclose one's personal items in a facade similar to a courthouse or bank building. Concrete, as the exterior treatment, lends the necessary touch of permanence and security. One might also view the chest structure as a reference to tomb architecture; wherein the coldness of the concrete facade is a suitable image.

elements involve the user in a pleasant fantasy of age and tradition. Whittlesey's education was in English literature and fine arts, and the structures are partly a canvas. He looks for boards that "take on the earmarks of family life." In true High Touch fashion, he likes pieces in which "old knots have fallen out, creating wonderful holes." His cupboards and dressers are available through the Gallery at Workbench.

Freestanding High Touch storage pieces are primarily one-of-a-kind. They include exhibition pieces designed for contests and personal visions influenced by the materials at hand.

It is High Touch to create curves instead of boxes, to combine woods and metals and plastics in the same piece of furniture. Compared with the contemporary preoccupation with glass and steel, with slick surfaces and with interchangeable modular pieces that can be stacked and used anywhere in the home, High Touch is in part a welcome return to a craft tradition.

Dick's Piece, a chest of drawers designed by the whimsical materials master from Texas, Carlton Cook, stands precariously on a High Touch/funky base of three bowling balls. Cook also employs black sponge rubber, ebonized wood, wire glass, and cue balls to make a storage piece that would probably stir up conversation and might need a psychologist to explain its "point."

LIGHTING

A High Touch glowing amoeboid blob of plastic could never have passed for a lighting fixture in Edison's day. Electric light was magical and so was technology, and consumers expected evidence of the mysteries. An enormous transformer and a bulky lamp base had to be there, or it wasn't really a lamp.

Early lighting fixtures were merely modifications of the same designs used for candles and gas, amalgams of handmade and machined fittings that were streamlined or baroque according to the style of the day. Ceramic bases became popular.

Today, technology has pared down the size of the light source to the point where it can be housed in a decorative shell only slightly larger than itself. The smaller source enables designers to create objects around and with the light source rather than having to conceal the dangerous "innards" of electrical lighting. Now when the shade is metal, it is because metal is

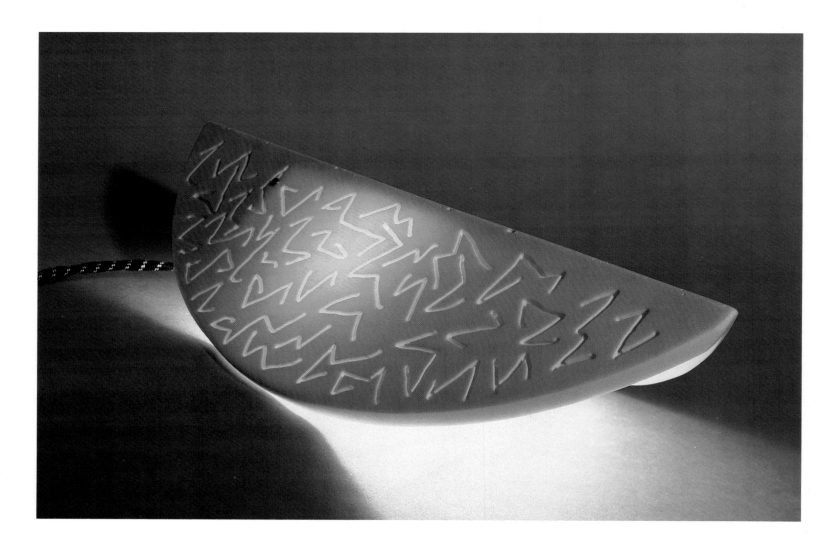

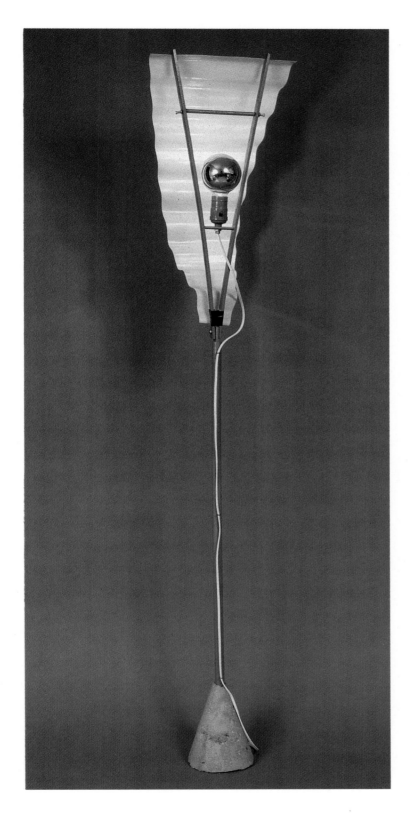

important to the designer's vision, not because it will protect the light bulb from the user.

We still need the magic. Lighting works in conjunction with interior architecture and furniture to embellish and enrich the visual experience, so the odd shapes and forms of lighting fixtures have echoed the prevailing design styles. Art Nouveau lamps were exemplified by ornamented creations from Tiffany, where both base and shade were works of art. Modernist

PAGE 59: *On-off,* a lamp design by David Zelman of New York, employs various machined metal parts in celebration of the industrial aesthetic. **LEFT, OPPOSITE:** In reaction to Dupont's touting of Corian's scratch-resistant surface, Leo Blackman has routed out an energetic pattern in the material for his *Rocking Lamp.* The pattern glows, demonstrating Corian's translucence. **LEFT:** With a corrugated fiberglass-sheet reflector/shade, the *Cyclops Lamp,* another Blackman design, stands on a base of concrete with a wooden broomstick supporting column.

ABOVE: Designer Jerry Van Deelen of New York City explores Corian's potential for translucence in a winged table lamp that has both incandescent and fluorescent light sources. He has added a rock crystal to one "wing," en-hancing the con-cern for light ef-fects. The Corian looks like a thin sheet of lit marble. The lamp was designed for a demonstration of Corian's design possibilities, sponsored by *Interiors* magazine and Dupont.

lamps celebrated the stark purity of line possible with metal cast in tubes and stamped into plates bent to direct rather than diffuse the light. Depression Modern gave us the flexible goose-necked lamp with its untippable cast-iron base.

So what can High Touch do for us? We have experienced the highly functional and the highly decorative. Our homes are cluttered with industrially sleek products whose simiplicity of form is a testament to the effectiveness of mass production. Even the most antique-oriented residence has rooms where antiques are overshadowed by Modernist streamlined products, finished entities that require no human interaction to bring them to aesthetic life.

High Touch has to bring back that feeling of participation in some new use of substance that demands admiration for the designer's inventiveness. Lighting in itself is a technological product, so High Touch designers are in reality reducing the impact of technology on the user. Most of the lighting designs shown here have less interest in exploiting technological advances than they have for appearance. Most of the designers are creating decorative objects that happen to be lighting, often simply using the most basic incandescent bulb. Materials for bases and shades are chosen for the effect they have on the light source and the composition of a room. The pieces are illuminated sculptures, where sculpture preempts utility.

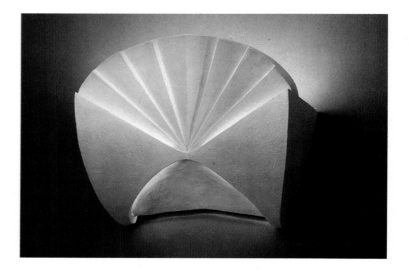

RIGHT: Kevin von Kluck, a Chicago-based furnishings and lighting designer, has formed hydrastone gypsum, a building construction material, into a sculptural wall sconce called the *Lotus.* The fixture is produced by the forward-thinking Boyd Lighting Company of San Francisco for the residential and commercial design market. **RIGHT, OPPOSITE:** The Furniture Club's *Planet* lamps are made of dyed concrete with light-directing, translucent shades made of rice paper. The light source is a standard incandescent bulb. Circular base element can be "rolled" into various positions to direct light up or toward a wall.

Lighting may be the High Touch product most accessible to the consumer. The sometimes revolutionary results explore the way materials react to light. Heat-resistant plastic ColorCore surfacing, as in Frank Gehry's *Fish Lamp*, is surprisingly translucent. Corian lit from behind reacts much like a thin sheet of alabaster or marble might, as shown in Jerry Van Deelen's Corian lamp. Leo Blackman's *Cyclops* lamp uses corrugated fiberglass as an effective diffuser and reactor. And neither Gehry nor Van Deelen has paid any attention to the traditional demands for base and shade; but each in a different way has created lamps where they are one and the same.

Where traditional forms are retained, the materials are odd choices: cement, galvanized metal, rubber tubing, and stove bolts. Charles Pfister's cast-concrete sconce directs light as well as any metal housing. Furniture Club simply uses concrete as a self-weighted base in rough and smooth textures. Ron Rezek eschews translucency for light directed by a bare-metal funnel and stove-pipe composition. His toylike lamp evokes thoughts of the Tin Man from *The Wizard of Oz*, and is enlivened by tiny square punchouts running along the rim of the shade.

When lamps are collages of found objects, the artist/designer seems to go out of his way to amuse. Leo Blackman's *Saucer Light* looks like a cross between a birthday cake on stilts and wheels of pleated paper. It alludes to its candle forebears with bobèches (small saucers used to catch wax drippings) on each of its three stiltlike supports.

Some High Touch lamps are Modernist with a twist of playfulness. A table lamp of brass with a brushed finish designed by Juergen Riehm, for example, is also a balance toy. By moving the copper ball at one end of the curved arm toward or away from the central axis, one moves the low-voltage halogen bulb down and up.

Kevin Walz reinvented the fire screen in a 40-inch square *Screen Light* with coppered-mesh screens and a sandblasted steel frame. Over an incandescent bulb,

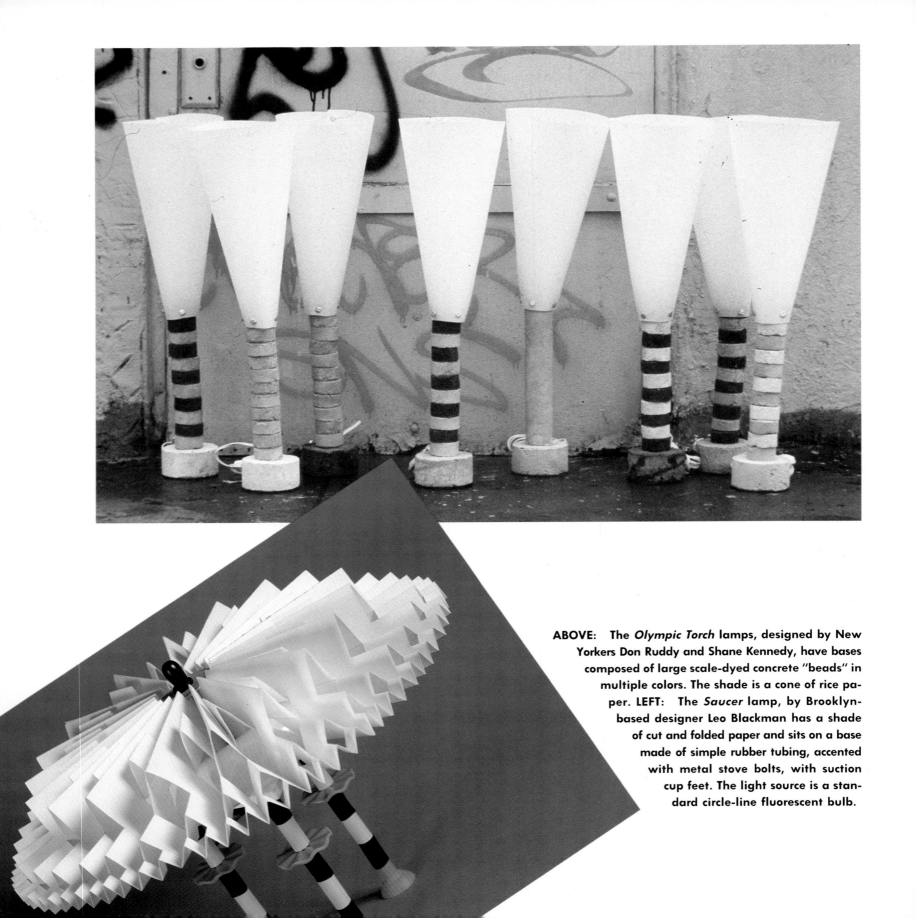

ABOVE: The *Olympic Torch* lamps, designed by New Yorkers Don Ruddy and Shane Kennedy, have bases composed of large scale-dyed concrete "beads" in multiple colors. The shade is a cone of rice paper. **LEFT:** The *Saucer* lamp, by Brooklyn-based designer Leo Blackman has a shade of cut and folded paper and sits on a base made of simple rubber tubing, accented with metal stove bolts, with suction cup feet. The light source is a standard circle-line fluorescent bulb.

ABOVE: Southern California architect and materials guru Frank Gehry has created *Fish Lamps,* exploring the once unknown translucent quality of Formica's ColorCore laminate product. Gehry tears the laminate into thin pieces, achieving a ragged and luminous-when-lit light sculpture.

the screens give a moire effect to the gentle ambient lighting. It is produced in limited runs for the Gallery of Applied Arts by Arc International.

There are also the lights that are made as sculpture. Neon, born as an industrial tool, has become a medium for expression. Many neon sculptures are simply art, but Lanna Longacres uses it to light pieces of porcelain, glass, and wood.

Lighting technology changes so rapidly that lighting manufacturers are in a continuing state of flux just to keep up with it, so they are not only willing to use new shapes, they require them. The shapes are available primarily through showrooms. But the nature of the industry is such that within a few years, any lamp successful at the designer level will either have been licensed to a mass-market manufacturer to be made in less expensive materials, or copied with just enough changes to deter copyright infringement suits.

Deelen. The shade is frosted Plexiglas draped with cotton gauze. Lamp base parts were found at secondhand shops and then reassembled. The accompanying picture frame shares the greenish oxidized-metal surface finish, and is a found object from Van Deelen's personal vault.

6

SETTINGS

Room design is an expression of personal taste and comfort. A High Touch room piles texture upon texture, and can be interpreted anew by each person who sees and experiences it. Materials-rich furniture can be the focal point of a room, or it can blend harmoniously into the background, depending on the use. High Touch materials have the ability to extend the compositional nature of interior design. Soft and hard, shiny and rusted, linear, curved, or jagged surfaces interact with each other and with light to create a specific mood and experience.

An advocate of novelty for its own sake might fill a room with unrelated High Touch pieces: a concrete chair, a Corian table, a fiberglass surfboard sofa, a vertical magazine rack, galvanized steel lighting fixtures, and aluminum accessories. And the result would most likely be a cacophony of overwhelming statements gibbering at each other, a menagerie of viewpoints. That does not mean, however, that using High Touch furniture is a delight best left only to those homeowners who can afford interior designers and architects to plan and orchestrate their interiors.

PAGE 73 AND ABOVE: Textile designer Scot Simon designed his own living/working loft in collaboration with Tim Button. It is a symphony of surface effects, involving ceramic tile, concrete, carpet, metal furnishings, and textural wall treatments. Paul Lu-

dick's *Apartheid Chair* is displayed in the manner of sculpture. LEFT, OPPOSITE: This bathroom by Kevin Walz is a study in the juxtaposition of textures. A wooden beam serves as the counter-top support and is a striking contrast to the sleek white tile.

Still, just as rooms designed by Mies van der Rohe demonstrate the ideal use of his Modernist furniture, so do the interiors of Kevin Walz and David Hertz illustrate the best approaches to effective High Touch room design.

Walz characteristically juxtaposes elements that carry their own histories—barn siding used as wall paneling, a carved chest, a Mexican straw chair—with the *tabula rasa* of new metal furniture. The multiplicity of textures play off each other in a visual composition, but most importantly, this restrained use of novelty engenders a feeling of continuity, a feeling very few designers of modern rooms have managed to evoke. No mere designer of bare sets, Walz creates rooms meant for living, rooms that look as if their occupants had just stepped out for a moment. He is not immune to the temptation of creating visual conceits. The slow convex curve of a shelf matches the concave curve on a metal bed frame, the placement of a table so the triangle formed by its legs repeats the angles of exposed ceiling beams. Yet this does not detract from the livability of his rooms.

Working within a Modernist framework, Alan Minar's interior space with bowed walls contrasts with

LEFT, OPPOSITE: In the loft bedroom of the Lanciani residence in New York, interior designer Kevin Walz introduces materials-aware touches in a subtle way. The visual experience is centered on the luxurious fabric of the bedspread. Its lushness is countered by the metal table, which has a raw appearance and simple geometry. **ABOVE:** A small, half-circular display shelf, also installed at the Lanciani loft, is made of concrete that lends a rich texture, especially when contrasted with the smooth walls.

RIGHT: The San Francisco architectural firm Batey and Mack designed the Kirlin residence in Northern California's Napa Valley, incorporating common, backyard-variety concrete construction blocks in the building of the fireplace wall. In addition, custom furniture pieces,

including a bed/lounge, seating elements, and a table share the textural concrete-block aesthetic. In a sense, this is a case of architects rediscovering a stereotyped material and breaking new ground with their appreciation and celebration of a now "new" material.

the hard and slick surfaces of furniture designed and chosen to fit the space. The Trump Tower apartment is almost an antithetic approach to the one used by Walz. The textures are in the curved walls of glass brick, the crinkled metallic paper ceiling, the simulated brushed-suede wallcovering. Space plays a crucial role in allowing the furniture to convey its individual messages, a home-as-museum-or-movie-set approach beloved by architects and highly effective in conjunction with modern furniture.

LEFT, OPPOSITE: This bedroom designed by interior designer Kevin Walz of New York features old and new elements that work together to produce an interior that is beautifully rich in sensory effect. Soft fabrics are used on the contrastingly hard-surfaced metal bed. A traditional wicker chair stands out when placed near a metal table. **ABOVE:** This bathroom from a Los Angeles residence designed by architect Fred Fisher features an unusual shower stall with walls of colored concrete block. The central column is a standard drainage tube.

LEFT, OPPOSITE: A metal-framed double bed, designed by Kevin Walz, is the centerpiece of the Harth residence bedroom, which features walls made of rough-hewn timber. Designer Walz often creates furniture for his projects.

David Hertz, too, manipulates space, using arched entries and a sweep of stairs to create rooms with an aura of intimacy often lacking in modern architecture. An angle within the arch intensifies the illusion with a suggestion of prehistoric caves or futuristic buildings. Rising above bleached-wood flooring to contrast with metal doors, the smooth cement archway repeats the curves of a cement-based table Hertz also designed. The play of materials is such that the High Touch and the Modernist complement each other.

One suspects Fred Fisher of studying Cubist paintings from the way he combines natural cement blocks and colored-tile ones inside and out in the Jorgenson home. In the bathroom, conventional ceramic tile, glass bricks, and shiny vertical metal fixtures add a decidedly surreal aspect. Throughout the interior Fisher employs the materials of industrial construction and leaves them unfinished. The cement block is porous; the columns are bare galvanized metal.

These surfaces will change with time, as over the years the environment or conditions change. The concrete will stain, grow darker with humidity, and get lighter in dry weather. Textures will wear; metals will rust. Each surface acquires the patina of use so admired in antique furniture and historic houses. That is part of the High Touch experience. As one grows older, so do the pieces of furniture and elements of construction, changing the visual experience in the same way a person ages.

Some High Touch pieces are far more subtle than

ABOVE: In an apartment at New York City's Trump Tower, furniture designers James Hong and Carmen Spera of New York worked in collaboration with interior designer Alan Minar of Florida. Pieces by Hong, Spera, and other furniture designers, including Forrest Myers, whose pink metal chairs are used in the dining area shown, are placed within a relatively neutral gray space. **RIGHT, OPPOSITE:** In this residence design by Los Angeles architect Michael Tolleson, the raw quality associated with High Touch is visible in the unfinished sheetrock walls. The architect designed most of the furnishings as well.

LEFT, OPPOSITE: With a shaped glass top mirroring the curve of the stairway under which it is placed, this concrete-based console table, by Los Angeles designer David Hertz, attempts to fit into a primarily traditional interior. ABOVE: In the Lessler residence, Los Angeles, Hertz is given free reign to incorporate concrete structures and furniture pieces. The tipped archway and walls make a textural statement; the dining table is a Hertz design surrounded by wooden-framed chairs. The combination of materials such as wood and concrete create light effects that are impossible using more "acceptable" treatments.

others. The easiest way to use High Touch pieces without enlisting professional help is to choose pieces that have a personal meaning and to combine them with what you already own, rather than trying for a room that screams out "design." The Memphis and Memphis-inspired furniture in the Beverly Hills mansion in Paul Mazursky's film *Ruthless People* was hideous in combination. But that was the intention, to reinforce a burlesque stereotype of people who have more money than taste.

LEFT, OPPOSITE: Architect Paul Segal puts corrugated fiberglass panels in a wooden structure, creating a dramatic indoor/outdoor room for a residence on Long Island. The material softens light and adds texture and color effects. **ABOVE:** The bathroom in artist Charles Arnoldi's Los Angeles home is austerely minimal thanks to the raw concrete wall and tub enclosure. **ABOVE, RIGHT:** Richly colored chair fabric sharply contrasts with the metal table by Kevin Walz.

High Touch is a reaction to the technological abyss of contemporary life. There is no need to overcompensate. It is perfectly all right to accept and enjoy mass-produced pieces. Life would be wearing if everything were required to elicit an emotional response.

Ironically, it is with the very designs that High Touch reacts against, Modernist architecture and furniture, that High Touch looks best. Those blank minimalist rooms that seem like empty stages waiting for drama welcome High Touch pieces.

7
OBJECTS

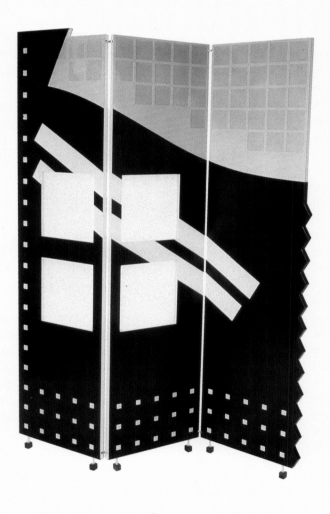

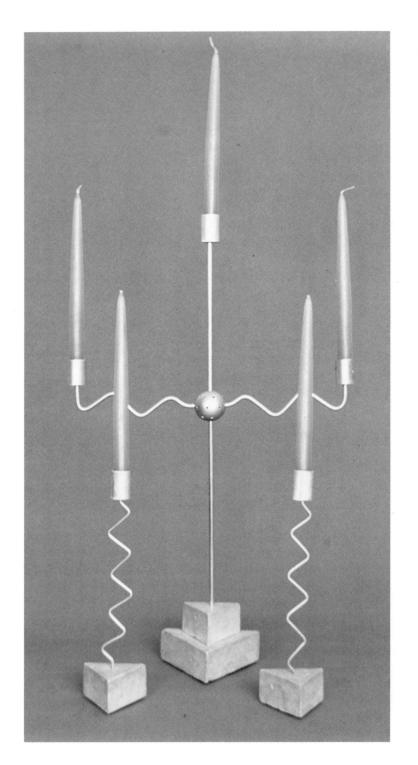

Little things *can* mean a lot. A purely minimalist room—with its serious, form-equals-function furniture—changes in character when the rug is patterned linoleum, the lamps are galvanized metal pipes, and the cement end tables hold candlesticks of oxidized copper cleverly bent and cut to resemble lizards. Accessories in a room are like spices in food: used judiciously, accessories help the contents of a room transcend the sum of their parts.

As a testament to its playfulness, High Touch asks these types of questions: Why can't the casing of a stereo system be cement? Why can't clockworks be housed in textured cement instead of finely finished wood or molded plastic? Why not replace stainless steel flatware with some made of brightly colored anodized aluminum? Why not have a watchband made from Astroturf?

PREVIOUS PAGE: This colorful folding screen made by James Schriber is composed of ColorCore, plywood, and Plexiglas. The translucent rectangles and the shadow of a mullioned window contained in the screen give it an added element of spatial depth. **LEFT:** Candlesticks by Jerry Kott of New York have zig-zagged aluminum supports and concrete bases, bringing materials-consciousness to the table top. **RIGHT, OPPOSITE:** A masterpiece of urban primitivism, the *Concrete Stereo System* designed by London's Ron Arad offers a sophisticated audio setup in a *Road Warrior*-inspired package.

LEFT, OPPOSITE: IOOA (The Interim Office for Architecture) is a San Francisco design firm founded by partners Bruce Tomb and John Randolph. One of the team's focuses is the reassessment of taken-for-granted, everyday objects and appliances, such as the household sink. Their version has a primitive, yet elegant appearance. Its basin is made of cast white bronze with a supporting structure of wood. ABOVE: New York artist Diana Vietor has fashioned an anodized aluminum flower vase that is reminiscent of the aluminum camping cups produced in the 1950s, but explores the material's application to a more elegant purpose. BE-LOW: Don Ruddy and Shane Kennedy's *Concrete Clocks* are cast in a clever wedge shape that allows them to stand firmly on a table or mantle. The concrete can be dyed in a selection of colors to coordinate with various interior schemes.

LEFT: An object designed for the interior can often have more to do with impact than actual use. In Ron Christensen's *Divider Room Divider*, a buyer would probably be more interested in the statement made about boundaries rather than the mundane division of a living space. The Atlanta-based designer uses the only material that can effectively create a rough and interior-alien surface—concrete. Barbed wire, in a series of x-shapes, furthers the theme of division. Layers of spray-painted graffiti transform the "screen" into a reminder of infamous political situations. For those whose homes serve as refuges from the real world, Christensen's piece is an unwelcome injection of reality. Harsh materials and surface treatments make the piece a severe version of High Touch.

These are all High Touch products and people are buying them. Accessories are minor investments, unlike furniture. The pieces are smaller, less of a shock to one's sensibilities, more of an invitation to join in on the humor. Accessories are the punctuation in an environmental essay.

In accessories design, the materials-minded artist is set free to knock over at will any ideas about the right and proper use of this material with that object. Accessories bridge the gap between functional object and art piece. They are admired for their beauty, wit, referents, content, and entertainment value.

A cement vase is witty: vases hold water and flowers, and cement is porous. This is a paradox the designer must overcome, and Furniture Club did so by lining the cement with glass.

Richard Nonas' pencil cup-as-paperweight cuts down on desk-top clutter and testifies to the weighty importance of its owner. The pencil cup and ashtray are welded raw steel and quite heavy.

High Touch transforms common materials and objects into something more unusual. For years, linoleum has been used on floors in lieu of vinyl because it is less expensive. A2Z gives new meaning to the material with its design and production of "hard rugs." They inlay tiles and pieces of tiles into linoleum in geometric patterns. These rugs, with tongue-in-cheek names such as *Navajoleum* and *File Friend*, are available at retail

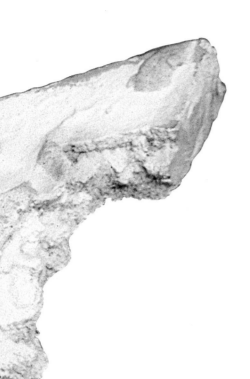

LEFT: Telecommunication in Bedrock is hard to come by. The choice of all those suburban-primitive Wilmas and Bettys is this concrete phone by Alex Locadia of New York. The design involves poured cement, gold leaf, and glass beads surrounding the innards of a modern phone. The cracked perimeter only adds to its novelty. Perhaps, the design is a commentary on a society where Snoopy, mallard ducks, fake classic volumes, and red lips serve as some of the mass-marketed "personality" phone offerings. Locadia almost takes a step backward here, transforming a modern convenience into a slightly worn, pretech statement. The buyer and user of such a telephone would have the private pleasure of knowing that when they "reached out and touched someone" it would be via an incredibly High Touch assemblage.

partnership, has embraced the aesthetic of this "lost" flooring material and created "rugs" consisting of various pieces of linoleum inlaid within a standard industrial mat border. Ries Niemi, Sheila Klein, and Norman Millar, the three partners of A2Z, see the rugs as practical and colorful alternatives to more typical fiber-rich floorcoverings. While one might find the linoleum a colder choice than wool or nylon carpet, the designers lend a homespun, one-of-a-kind quality to the material, creating an overall visual effect similar to the feel and look of homemade quilts or American Indian blankets. Shown also are cube tables constructed by A2Z that are covered in inlaid linoleum pieces, as well. The colorful cubes, like the rugs, fit into the homemaker's dream of easy maintenance. When a spill occurs, there is no need to reach for the furniture polish. Instead, one can just grab a mop and some Spic-N-Span.

and by custom order. Another example is artist Alex Locadia's concrete stereo. He describes why it is important for it to be different from a regular stereo, saying, "Encasing state-of-the-art electronics in concrete makes what is normally an average experience a special one. That becomes a form of communication."

ColorCore may be *the* plastic for High Touch, as it is used for everything from desk surfaces to jewelry and lamps, from the prosaic to the frivolous. John Bailey created desk accessories called *Colorcoordinates* by layering ColorCore and cutting it into clean shapes. The shapes have been seen before, but the pure-color-through-and-through material gives the concept a new validity.

Even though an item may be designed for mass production, the goal in High Touch is to have it appear unique, as if it were *not* mass-produced.

ABOVE: This decorative bowl by Chris Collicott of Los Angeles consists of oxydized copper, brass, and concrete elements. **NEAR RIGHT, OPPOSITE:**   Salad servers, made by Kirsten Hawthorne of New York, are fun and functional. They are made of sanded and cut acrylic sheet with brass studs. **FAR RIGHT, OPPOSITE:**   Paris-based designer Patrick Naggar echoes the primitive aesthetic in his decorative screen, but uses a combination of modern materials to achieve the look. The screen's frame is constructed from fiberglass rods and is supported on a base of polished steel with nylon wheels. Panels are made of gold-leafed paper. The "native" touch is provided by horsehair tassels up top. Naggar combines industrial and fragile materials for a striking interior embellishment.

Wearables

Trends in fashion so often presage trends in furniture design that one cannot be surprised to find the same High Touch materials applied to wearables. Jewelry that uses bits of Pirelli rubber, stainless steel, anodized metals, plastic laminates, or Corian is common in High Touch.

The designers of High Touch wearables appeal to those consumers who seek out the unique, the unusual, even the unusable. Their designs are experimental, alternately charming and overwhelming the viewer by their audacity. High Touch jewelry and clothing, like furniture, are tactile in their expression. How a designer masks or celebrates a material's texture is very important. And because the probable reaction of the consumer is to try on the piece to see how it "feels" as well as how it looks, the materials-rich wearable succeeds from the start, for it involves the wearer.

BELOW: The monumentality of concrete has been brought down to an intimate scale in Alex Locadia's wristwatch design; the band is made of Astroturf.

LEFT, OPPOSITE: Armlet by New York City-based jewelry designer Thomas Gentille is made of Formica Corporation's Color-Core solid-colored laminate, acrylic, and brass studs.
ABOVE: The exciting color effect of Ivy Ross's woven bracelet is caused by the material used—Niobium. The light-reactive surface of the piece is a result of electrically charging the metal. The bracelet also contains oxydized copper elements.

Wearing a bracelet of the same material as your kitchen counter could be a social statement or simply recognition of the beauty of the new plastics. In jewelry, new materials engender new designs, and a material becomes new when removed from its normal context. For High Touch jewelry, pieces of sponge, metal screening, papier-mâché, and painted construction paper take the place of precious stones and precious metals, and bright colors and unusual shapes only intensify the effect.

Thomas Mann's techno-romantic jewelry is made from the inner workings of technology, the tiny cogs, wheels, and fittings that can so easily put electronic gadgetry out of commission if they jog loose. These in-comprehensible parts are transformed through Mann's vision into jewelry even a techno-phobe can appreciate.

ColorCore plastic surfacing has inspired wildly diverse applications. Cliff Furnald bent the material into a wide cuff bracelet accented by controlled chippings, and Ann Scott cut and bent sinuous curves for a light-weight collar/necklace.

Materials taken out of context are as important an element in design here as anywhere in High Touch. Earrings made from pieces of metal lunch boxes that mysteriously show an eye, part of a cape, or other bits of the hero depicted and are complemented by copper rivets are only one example.

Ivy Ross and Bob Ebendorf often collaborate on

LEFT: Wendy Stevens designed these evening bags, combining suede, nickel silver, brass, and copper. The hard-edged geometric forms have a somewhat industrial aesthetic, due to the use of riveted joints. The East Village-based designer was inspired by the rivets seen on the exterior of the subway cars of New York City's Transit Authority and incorporated them into the delicate evening-bag design vocabulary.

as gold and pearl and accents of rare niobium, but his philosophy of design could be the thread underlying all High Touch jewelry. "I use the human form as a stage. I try to adorn with drama, flattering the wearer while intriguing the viewer."

Fashion is probably the most High Touch statement a person ever makes, but High Touch fashion is unlikely to be found in retail stores aside from boutiques. There are exceptions. A form of High Touch actually

ABOVE: For their *Cobblestone Series*, New York jewelry designers Joanna and Davi Ruisi-Besares use hand-dyed paper and overlay it on brass, mimicking the look of small stones strung together to create bracelets, earrings, and necklaces. Some pieces are further ornamented with an inlay of metal. In their use of papier-mâché, the jewelry makers are, in a sense, creating three-dimensional trompe l'oeil.

jewelry design, creating pieces with a sense of delicacy and scale often absent in contemporary work. Ross's father was an industrial designer who used to bring home pieces of work in progress, which may explain why Ross leaps so eagerly into exploring new materials. She gets aggravated by designers who call their work jewelry when it can't be worn, "Jewelry design is akin to industrial design because you have to be aware of the neck, arm, and body."

Alan Revere stays with conventional materials such

BELOW: A pin by New York City's Ivy Ross is a symphony of High Touch materials. Formica ColorCore surfacing material, titanium strands, and inlaid wood are combined here.

ABOVE: A *Bead Necklace*, designed by Ivy Ross and Robert Ebendorf, a jewelry-making team from New York City, elevates ColorCore surfacing material and rubber to the level of silver and brass, the two metals with which they are combined here.

made its way into Bloomingdale's. Belts made of pieces of silk drapery ties, upholstery trimmings, and metallic findings, they were accented with bits of shell, bone, feathers, and cast-acrylic plastic. This unlikely mélange of textures was combined with color and style that made one want to touch and explore each belt. The grommets, studs, rivets, and metal studs seen in ones and twos on jeans and government-issue rainwear and in profusion on the jackets of punks have been adopted by the mass-market clothing manufacturers.

Need the materials be new for the design to be High Touch? Sometimes the way an item is made and the message it conveys are enough. For example, Mark Mahall's chain-store gold vinyl bomber's jacket with fake-fur lining is covered with 25,000 brass safety pins. The pins take an organic and twisting path, crossing and linking, alive and tactile.

High Touch wearables announce themselves to the world, defying one to wear them at the same time they invite being worn. It's fashion that goes almost too far, and clearly enjoys it.

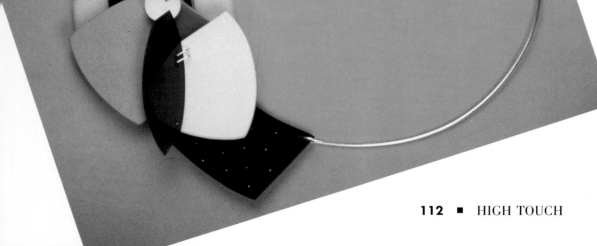

LEFT: Alice Klein's ColorCore-rich choker necklace uses the material in the same manner as a more conventional jewelrymaker would use pieces of jade or ivory. **RIGHT, OPPOSITE:** Winner of a *Diamond Today* award, Ivy Ross's square pin of colorful titanium strands and vibrantly hued diamonds is a statement of the New Jewelry aesthetic, where materials of unequal status are combined in innovative and striking ways.

SOURCES

ADDESSO
199 Boylston Street
Chestnut Hill, MA 02167
617-451-2212

AMBIENTI
310 South Catalina Avenue
Redondo Beach, CA 90277
213-376-0447

ART ET INDUSTRIE
594 Broadway
New York, NY 10013
212-431-1661

ATELIER INTERNATIONAL
30-20 Thompson Avenue
Long Island City, NY 11101
718-392-0300

A2Z
5526 West Pico Boulevard
Los Angeles, CA 90019
213-937-2072

THE CARLTON COOK COMPANY
1715 West 26th Street
Houston, TX 77008
713-880-1122

CHIASSO
13 East Chestnut Street
Chicago, IL 60610
312-642-2808

CITY
213 West Institute Place
Chicago, IL 60610
312-664-9581

CIVILISATION
78 Second Avenue
New York, NY 10003
212-254-3788

**CLODAGH,
ROSS AND WILLIAMS**
122 Saint Marks Place
New York, NY 10009
212-505-1774

CONTREJOUR
190 Columbus Avenue
New York, NY 10023
212-877-7900

DI-ZIN
2430 Main Street
Santa Monica, CA 90405
213-392-9806

DOT ZERO
165 Fifth Avenue
New York, NY 10010
212-533-8322

EKLEKTIKA
The Bakery Center
5701 Sunset Drive
South Miami, FL 33143
305-667-0788

**FURNITURE
OF THE TWENTIETH CENTURY**
227 West 17th Street
New York, NY 10011
212-929-6023

THE GALLERY AT WORKBENCH
470 Park Avenue South
New York, NY 10016
212-481-5454

GALLERY 91
91 Grand Street
New York, NY 10013
212-966-3722

THE GALLERY OF THE APPLIED ARTS
24 West 57th Street
New York, NY 10019
212-765-3560

GILES & LEWIS
464 Columbus Avenue
New York, NY 10024
212-362-5330

HOKIN/KAUFMAN GALLERY
210 West Superior
Chicago, IL 60610
312-266-1211

HOT HOUSE
345 West Broadway
New York, NY 10013
212-966-7978

INTERNA DESIGNS
6-168 Merchandise Mart
Chicago, IL 60654
312-467-6076

JANIS
200 West Superior
Chicago, IL 60610
312-280-5357

GEORGE KOVACS
330 East 59th Street
New York, NY 10022
212-838-3400

LIMN
457 Pacific Avenue
San Francisco, CA 94133
415-397-7474

DENNIS MILLER ASSOCIATES
72 Fifth Avenue
New York, NY 10011
212-242-7842

NEOPHILE
1239 Broadway
New York, NY 10001
212-213-9313

NEW CITY EDITIONS
525 Venezia
Venice, CA 90291
213-822-0818

NEW LiVING
6812 Melrose Avenue
Los Angeles, CA 90038
213-933-5553

KEISER NEWMAN
134 N. 3rd Street
Philadelphia, PA 19106
215-923-7438

NOLTE
110 Wooster Street
New York, NY 10013
212-431-0162

PROPS
3001 Hennipen Avenue South
Minneapolis, MN 55408
612-823-6467

ROGERS-TROPEA, INC.
1351 Third Avenue
New York, NY 10021
212-249-8310

SPATIAL ENVIRONMENTAL ELEMENTS LTD.
118 Spring Street
New York, NY 10012
212-683-3188

SQUARE ONE L.A.
3806 Beverly Boulevard
Los Angeles, CA 90048
213-275-6683

STATE OF THE ART
47 Greenwhich Avenue
New York, NY 10014
212-924-8973

SYNDESIS STUDIO
1708 Berkeley Street
Santa Monica, CA 90404
213-829-9932

URBAN OBJECTS
1724 Sansom Street
Philadelphia, PA 19103
215-557-9474

BIBLIOGRAPHY

Articles:

Beals, Kathie. "Neon Serves as Novel Link of Art and Light." *Reporter Dispatch*, 1 February 1987.

Castle, Wendell. "The Leading Edge." *Popular Mechanics*, November 1986, 78–90.

Giovanni, Joseph. "At Show, Radical Furniture is Tamed." *New York Times*, 4 April 1985, C1+.

Hammel, Lisa. "Angles, Steeples and Other Presences." *American Craft*, December 1986/January 1987, 30–37.

Haney, Laura J. "Furniture's Greatest Unknown Designer." *Upholstering Industry*, July/August 1977, 10–11.

"New and Notable." *ID Magazine of International Design*, January/February 1987, 62–65.

"Portfolio." *American Craft*, February/March 1987.

"Sculptural Intent." *American Craft*, August/September 1986, 32–33.

Slavin, Maeve. "Working it Out." *Interiors*, September 1985.

Vilades, Pilar. "All 4 One." *Progressive Architecture*, September 1986, 107–9.

Wissinger, Joanna. "Artful Craft." *Progressive Architecture*, September 1986, 107–9.

Exhibition Catalogs:

Furniture by Architects. Cambridge: MIT/Hayden Gallery, 1981.

Material Evidence: New color techniques in handmade furniture. Washington, D.C.: Smithsonian Institution, 1985.

Material Pleasures: Furniture for a postmodern age. Queens, N.Y.: The Queens County Art and Cultural Center, 1985.

Books:

Dale, Julie Schafler. *Art to Wear.* New York: Abbeville Press, 1986.

DiNoto, Andrea. *Art Plastic.* New York: Abbeville Press, 1985.

Domergue, Denise. *Artists Design Furniture.* New York: Harry N. Abrams, 1984.

Forty, Adrian. *Objects of Desire: Design and society from Wedgewood to IBM.* New York: Warner Books, 1982.

Grief, Martin. *Depression Modern.* New York: Universe Books, 1975.

Hine, Thomas. *Populuxe.* New York: Alfred A. Knopf, 1986.

Knackstedt, Mary V., and Laura J. Haney. *Profitable Career Options for Designers.* New York: Kobro Publications, 1986.

Kron, Joan, and Suzanne Slesin. *High-Tech.* New York: Clarkson N. Potter, 1978.

Meadmore, Clement. *The Modern Chair.* New York: Van Nostrand Reinhold, 1979.

Naisbitt, John. *Megatrends: Ten New Directions Transforming Our Lives.* New York: Warner Books, 1982.

Page, Marian. *Furniture Designed by Architects.* New York: Whitney Library of Design, 1980.

Rybczynski, Witold. *Home: A Short History of an Idea.* New York: Viking, 1986.

Sembach, Klaus-Jurgen. *Contemporary Furniture.* New York: Architectural Book Publishing, 1982.

Tate, Allen, and C. Ray Smith. *Interior Design in the 20th Century.* New York: Harper & Row, 1986.

INDEX

A

A2Z, 57, 98, 101
Aalto, Alvar, 15, 27
Accessories, 92–102
Adams, Hank, 43
Adams, Jay, 3, 35, 38, 45
Aluminum, use of, 3
Ambasz, Emilio, 6
Antiques, interest in, 2
Arad, Ron, 92
Arc International, 9, 27, 66, 98
Arnoldi, Charles, 89
Art Nouveau lamps, 61

B

Baekland, Leo, 5
Bailey, John, 102
Bakelite, 5
Batey and Mack, 78–79
Bauhaus school, 4, 20–21
Becker, Hermann, 9
Blackman, Leo, 3, 61, 64, 65, 66
Bohlin, Jonas, 24, 48, 51
Bonetti/Garouste, 34
Bow Wow House, 45
Breuer, Marcel, 4, 21
Buchsbaum, Alan, 41
Button, Tim, 75

C

Calatroni, Sergio, 23
Castle, Wendall, 39–40
Ceremonial seating, 13, 14–20
Chairs. *See* Seating
Christensen, Ron, 49, 51, 55, 97
Clothing, 104, 108–12
Cockrell, John, 32
Collicott, Chris, 98, 102
Colombo, Joe, 5, 48

ColorCore, 7–8, 13, 26, 39–41, 49, 51, 64, 92, 102, 104, 107, 109, 111, 112
Comfort, seating, 27
Concrete, use of, 3, 35–38
Cook, Carlton, 32, 38, 57
Corian, 7, 35, 61, 62
Craft tradition, return to, 8, 57
Crystal Palace, 6

D

Depression Modern lamps, 63
Designers, 8–9
DMI, 5
Duke, Joe, 9

E

Eames, Charles, 2, 5, 27, 48
Eames, Ray, 2, 5
Ebendorf, Robert, 107–8, 111
Economics, technological advances and, 7
Ergonomic seating, 14

F

Fashion, 108–12
Fisher, Fred, 81, 84
Formica Corporation, 7–8
Frost, Myra and Geoffrey, 37
Functional art, 4
Function-oriented seating, 13, 14
Furnald, Cliff, 107
Furniture, 2, 3, 4–8. *See also* Seating; Storage; Tables
Furniture Club, 3, 9, 35, 37, 38, 41, 49, 64, 98
Furry-mushroom fad, 5

G

Gallery at Workbench, 57

Gallery of Applied Arts, 66
Gehry, Frank, 64, 67
Gentille, Thomas, 105

H

Harth residence, 83
Hawthorne, Kirsten, 102
Helzer, Richard, 44
Herman Miller Inc., 5
Hertz, David, 15, 27, 34, 41, 77, 83, 87
Higgins, Dennis, 51, 54
High Tech design, 5–6
High Touch
    defining, 1–4
    designers, 8–9
    material precedents of, 4–8
Holl, Steven, 20, 27
Hong, James, 84

I

Interior design, 2, 73–89
IOOA (Interim Office for Architecture), 95

J

Jackson, Elizabeth Browning, 3, 9, 26–27
Jewelry, 104–8, 111
Jorgenson home, 84

K

Kane, Brian, 3, 9, 25, 27
Kartell chairs, 5
Keiser, Bruce, 31, 34, 35
Kennedy, Shane, 3, 37, 41, 66, 95
Kirlin residence, 78–79
Klein, Alice, 112
Klein, Shiela, 54, 101

Kluck, Kevin von, 64
Knoll, Florence, 48
Kott, Jerry, 92
Kron, Joan, 6

L

Lamps. *See* Lighting
Lanciani residence, 77
Larimore, Jack, 13
Le Corbusier, 8
Lessler residence, 87
Lighting, 59–71
Linoleum rugs, 98
Locadia, Alex, 98–102, 100, 105
Longacres, Lanna, 66
Lucite, 5
Ludick, Paul, 3, 19, 20, 27, 41, 75

M

Mahall, Mark, 112
Main, Terence, 31, 34
Mann, Thomas, 107
Marcoux, John, 45
Maruyama, Wendy, 43, 49, 51
Material precedents of High Touch, 4–8
Materials
    for jewelry, 107–8
    seating, 24–27
    for tables, 30–44
Materials-rich design, 2–3
Memphis, 7, 88
Mercatali, Davide, 17
Mies van der Rohe, Ludwig, 4, 8, 16, 77
Millar, Norman, 54, 101
Minar, Alan, 77–80, 84
Modernist lamps, 61–63
Murphy, Brian A., 6
Myers, Forrest, 3, 24, 27, 41, 84

N

Naggar, Patrick, 27, 32, 38–39, 102
Naisbitt, John, 2
Nelson, George, 48
Neon, 66

New Jewelry aesthetic, 112
Newman, Don, 31, 34, 35
Niemi, Ries, 54, 101
Nonas, Richard, 3, 98
Norskag, Jody, 21, 27

O

Objects, 91–112
    accessories, 92–102
    wearables, 104–12

P

Patina of use, 84
Paxton, Joseph, 6
Pedrizettio, Paolo, 17, 27
Peed, Jim, 5
Peregalli, Davide, 27
Peregalli, Maurizio, 17, 23, 27
Pfister, Charles, 3, 9, 64, 68
Pierschalla, Michael, 13, 27
Plastics, age of, 5
Postmodern design, 6
Postmodern Neoclassical design, 7

R

Rand, Ayn, 8
Randolph, John, 37, 95
Revere, Alan, 108–9
Rex Designs, 3, 38
Rezek, Ron, 9, 41, 64, 68
Riehm, Juergen, 3, 65, 71
Robertson, M. Clark, 5
Robinson, Robert, 13, 27
Room design, 73–89
Ross, Ivy, 9, 105, 107–8, 109, 111, 112
Rubber, use of, 3, 111
Ruddy, Don, 3, 37, 41, 66, 95
Rugs, linoleum, 98
Ruisi-Besares, Joanna and Davi, 108

S

Schriber, James, 92

Scott, Ann, 107
Seating, 5, 11–27
Segal, Paul, 89
Settings, 73–89
Simon, Scot, 75
Slesin, Suzanne, 6
Spera, Carmen, 84
Stanger, Jay, 53
Steel, use of, 3
Stein, Sherry, 21, 27
Stevens, Wendy, 107
Storage, 47–57

T

Tables, 29–45
Techno-romantic jewelry, 107
Tese, Carl, 31
Tigerman, Stanley, 13, 24–26
Tolleson, Michael, 84
Tomb, Bruce, 37, 95
Tradition, return to, 2
Trump Tower apartment, 80, 84
Tubular steel, use of, 4–5, 20–21

V

Van Deelen, Jerry, 62, 64, 71
Venturi, Robert, 7
Viemeister, Tucker, 3–4, 20, 27
Vietor, Diana, 95

W

Walsh, Michael, 32, 35
Walz, Kevin, 65–66, 75, 77, 81, 83, 89
Wearables, 104–12
Whittlesey, Stephen, 51–57
Whyte, William H., 13
Wright, Frank Lloyd, 8

Z

Zelman, David, 61
Zeus group, 17, 23, 24, 27